Growth makes
you happy

GROWTH

Peter De Keyzer

An Optimist's View
of Progress
and the Free Market

MAKES

YOU HAPPY

LANNOO

www.lannoo.com

Register on our website and we will send you
a regular newsletter with information about new books
and interesting, exclusive offers.

Cover design: Studio Lannoo
Layout: Steven Theunis & Olu Vandenbussche, Armée de Verre
Translation: Irene Schaudies
Cover Image: Carrie Mill

Second Edition
© Uitgeverij Lannoo nv, Tielt, 2013 and Peter De Keyzer
D/2014/45/445
NUR 781/160
02898

To Marleen and Hans
My mother and brother – because they helped make me who I am today.

To Karen
My wife – my support, my companion and the love of my life forever.

To Jens and Stef
My children – for whom it all has yet to begin.

To a wonderful, happy, better future for all.

Table of contents

Introduction

Looking out the window of an airplane
at the port of Antwerp slowly sliding by.

It happens a couple of times a year and every time it's a special expe
rience. It's also the most concise summary of why I wanted to write
this book.

A port represents two things. In the first place it stands for the way
human beings make use of their natural surroundings – waterways,
tides, geography – in order to improve their lot. A port is not a work of
art, nor is it a religious symbol; it is the quintessential metaphor for
the innovative, economic human being, who uses the environment
to advantage. It is a metaphor for humanity as it becomes wealthier, happier and more affluent by pursuing its enlightened self-interest. In the second place, a port is a symbol of the free market and
globalization. It is a passageway to the rest of the world and perhaps
the most visible meeting place of supply and demand. Thousands of
colorful containers carrying mixed cargo, raw materials, fruit, automobiles, sport shoes or replacement parts for machines: they are all
part of the chain of value in a globalized world economy. Nowhere is
the interaction between supply and demand in a free market more
visible than in a port. Here the individual demands of billions of
individual consumers for energy, transportation, food, clothing,
luxury, communication and information encounter the craftsman-
ship, labor, innovation and entrepreneurship of millions of different
suppliers. In a free market, demands from China and Belgium find
supplies from Germany and the United States. In a port, the apparently invisible confrontation of supply and demand comes to the
surface in a spectacular way. A port is thus a free market crystallized:

9

now and since the beginning of human history, it has always been the most efficient way to improve the wealth of an entire society.

The airplane itself is also a double metaphor. In the first place it stands for humanity's victory over nature. The thinking, innovative human being, who continually succeeds in overcoming the limitations of the environment. No victory was ever greater or more important than humanity's victory over gravity. Since the origin of the species, the dream of flight has been inextricably bound to humankind. Two American brothers realized this dream at the beginning of the 20th century on the beach at Kitty Hawk. Airplanes are also the most tangible proof of humanity's ability to realize its dreams. Humanity is capable of freeing itself from earthly limitations and obstacles, of rising above itself. This capacity for surmounting obstacles is uniquely human, but today all too frequently underestimated. The second metaphor is the unique perspective afforded by an airplane: it adds dimension and helps one to see broader connections. This too is an essential part of this story about growth.

A broad overview of technological progress, prosperity, and the free market – that's this book in a nutshell. *Growth Makes You Happy* is in the first place a reaction to the current double pessimism surrounding economic growth. Today, there are two opposed forms of growth pessimism: one is concerned with lack of growth, the other with too much growth.

The first group of growth pessimists is worried about the current economic standstill in Belgium, Europe or the West generally. They ask themselves whether and to what degree we will still be able to create additional wealth. Pessimism about sputtering growth, faulty decision-making, high taxes, political cacophony, a lack of entrepreneurship, and an environment that is hostile to business – all of these common concerns will pass revue. Nothing is more corrosive for a society and for political stability than a long-term period of stagnating or even decreasing wealth. It increases voters' resistance to change; it makes social and political compromise more difficult; and it makes social relations tense. In a world in which prosperity does not grow, the progress of one always comes at the expense of another. A society without growth and with no hope of improvement starts to come apart at the seams. The paradox is that things have never been better than they are today: we are older, healthier, richer and enjoy more social and political equality than ever before. Yet today, we seem more concerned with keeping what we have than trying to achieve what is still possible. We are champions in distributing wealth, but we are gradually forgetting how to create it.

The second group of growth pessimists complains of the exact opposite: an excess of growth. This school of pessimists is afraid that we focus too much on growth and progress. That the planet will soon implode under the pressure of eleven billion inhabitants. That we are collectively causing the planet to overheat, that we will cut down the very last tree and haul the last fish gasping from the ocean. These are the people who constantly remind us of our ecological footprint and global warming, who constantly bombard us with the message that we are all running ourselves silly in the rat race of economic growth. This kind of pessimist always looks for the limitations and never for the possibilities. This book has a number of answers for them as well.

In part one we start with the free market and examine the reasons why this engine of prosperity is still the most efficient way to make as many people possible as wealthy as possible. Then we look at why intervening in the free market is a bad idea: good intentions often have unintended consequences. Minimum pricing and maximum pricing both reduce the total amount of wealth. There is one important exception: in the case of pollution or the exhaustion of the climate or raw materials, government intervention is needed in order to maintain prosperity at acceptable levels.

In the second part of the book we will examine the theme of economic growth and progress in more depth. We will show that growth is actually a fairly recent phenomenon. For the better part of human history, people were poor and economic growth non-existent. It was the 'discovery' of economic growth that saved us from our miserable existence. Next we devote an entire chapter to the fear that too great an increase in the global population and economy will cause the earth to implode. The argument that the continual disappearance of industries and jobs is harming our prosperity will also be refuted. Turbulence, change and revolution are, after all, part of the process of innovation, entrepreneurship and economic growth. In the last part we will focus, first and foremost, on the obstacles to economic growth. Why is it so difficult for us to grow today? Demography, debts, the Euro-crisis, an addiction to the status quo, an aversion to risk ... each will be considered in turn. In the penultimate chapter, we present a number of major principles needed to reconnect with the creation of wealth. By way of a conclusion, in the final chapter a growth optimist will summarize his arguments in an imagined conversation with a growth pessimist.

In this way, this book seeks to offer an answer to those who think we cannot live without sufficient growth, as well as those who think we will not survive too much growth. The answer to both parties is largely the same: we need more free market, more belief in progress and technology, and more belief in the future. Hence, this book is also a plea in favor of more optimism, more risk, more individualism, less collectivism and more freedom.

Peter De Keyzer

CHAPTER 1

The free market as the engine of prosperity

"Greed is good." — **Gordon Gekko**, main character in the 1987 film *Wall Street*, played by Michael Douglas

"It is not for the benevolence of the butcher, the brewer or the baker that we can expect our dinner, but from their regard to their self-interest." — **Adam Smith**, philosopher and forefather of economics (1723-1790)

What do prehistoric Australia, a playground full of students and a prisoner-of-war camp have in common? And what does a Soviet leader's visit to a supermarket in San Francisco have to do with it?

Australia, the playground and the prisoner-of-war camp are all places where spontaneous markets come into existence. Of course, we are not talking about markets in the classic sense, with tradesmen in stalls peddling their wares in exchange for money. In fact, in all other examples of how markets function this is rarely the case. Nor are we usually dealing with trade in the classic sense of the word, in which products or services are sold for a particular price. It could just as well be about agreements to work together, an exchange of goods for other goods or an exchange of goods in return for providing services in the future, and so on.

In Australia, evidence has been found to suggest that the original inhabitants already engaged in trade thousands of years ago. Aboriginals from the north of Australia were specialized in making spears with barbs collected from the tails of stingrays. The tribes that lived deep inland made sharp axes with stones from the surrounding environment. The two tribes had no mutual contact and did not trade with one another directly. However, the Aboriginals on the coast exchanged their spears with neighboring tribes who lived further inland. These tribes in turn used the spears as a medium of exchange in their trade with other tribes. In this way, a long chain of bartering came into existence. To the south – in the direction inland – for spears; to the north – in the direction of the coast – for axes. And so it seems that Aboriginals deep in the Bush had spears with stingray barbs, and their fellow tribesmen on the coast had axes that came from inland. From these trade patterns it even appears that the spears were scarcer the farther inland one went. Inland, spears were priced higher than on the coast. Axes, by contrast, were 'more expensive' on the coast than in the inland.

The trade and market in spears and axes in prehistoric Australia arose in a society without writing, without government, without written laws, without courts, without science. Engaging in trade is so deeply embedded in our human nature that it is older than nearly all other human institutions.

In camps where prisoners of war were detained during the Second World War, markets of a sort also came into being. The American professor Robert A. Radford has described his experiences in a German prisoner-of-war camp and explains how a market came into existence spontaneously.

In the camp, aid packages from the International Red Cross were distributed on a regular basis. In addition to food, they also contained several packs of cigarettes. The prisoners who didn't smoke could use their cigarettes as a medium of exchange in order to get more food, extra soap or even to have their clothes mended. The Sikhs in the camp wanted to exchange their beef for other products. The French, in turn, appeared to be more interested in coffee. Several prisoners put up a sheet of paper in the common areas of the camp which listed the products they had on offer and the products they wanted in return – a sort of eBay *avant la lettre*, and that in wartime. After a while, a real market was created. Not because it had been imposed from the outside, nor because some institution or other decided it would be a good idea, but because it was the best way for everybody to improve his own situation.

Similarly, on every average playground, several markets crop up spontaneously among the students. Who doesn't remember the trade in baseball cards around the time of a big game? Even at an early age, children quickly learn the value of a rare sports card with a picture of a famous baseball player, an unusual marble or a playing card with special characteristics. Whether they are paid for in kind, with candy or even pocket money: the relative price of that which is scarce is systematically driven up.

The preceding examples illustrate the first important observation: the free market, trade and supply and demand were not invented by anyone. On the contrary, they are deeply embedded in our human nature. That we are all free individuals, each with specific needs, desires, preferences and tastes can be summed up in no better way than the creation of a market. It is only because our needs differ from those of other people that we want to engage in trade. If all the prisoners of war in the camp had enjoyed smoking, eating beef or drinking coffee, there would have been no need for bartering or trade. That our needs and capacities are completely different defines us as human beings. I think; therefore I am. We are individuals; therefore we trade.

A unique characteristic of the free market is that it provides a win-win situation for both parties. The pack of cigarettes that is bartered for coffee, the Aboriginal who trades an axe for a pair of spears, the card with your favorite baseball hero that are given away in exchange for a lot of other cards: in every case, the transaction comes about because both parties see it as a good deal. Both find that they are better off than before the barter, exchange or sale.

Buying bread from the baker. Hiring a new employee. Having a mechanic fix your car. Buying a painting from an upcoming artist. Mowing the neighbor's grass, in return for which he helps paint your house. Selling a signed Elvis Presley record to a fervent collector. Preparing the menu du jour for a packed restaurant. In all of these cases both parties to the transaction have become happier or wealthier than before the transaction. The one who supplies or sells and the one who demands or buys.

Every time we engage in trade with one another, we increase our wealth. Not only our own, but also that of society as a whole. This is also evident from worldwide indicators of freedom in general and freedom to participate in trade specifically. The more free people are to trade with one another and to pursue their enlightened self-interest, the greater their prosperity.

The concept 'free market' is a double one. A free market presumes the existence of people who want to exchange goods or services of their own free will. But if one of the parties does not have free will, there is no market. In the best case there is exploitation or compulsion, in the worst, theft.

The Fraser Institute has for decades maintained figures relating to the economic freedom of the world. In this way, they are able to measure the degree to which trade and the functioning of the market are fostered or hindered in a large number of countries. They also examine the level of taxation, the existence of an independent judiciary, opportunities for international trade, regulation of the labor market, and the degree of corruption and administrative burden. From these figures it is abundantly clear that greater economic freedom is associated with greater prosperity and greater economic growth.

Illustration 1: **Economic freedom and income per capita**
Source: Fraser Institute, 2012

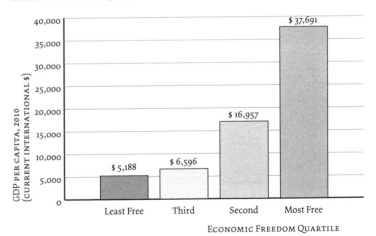

17

How wealth is distributed or what has to be done with it is a choice that every society must make for itself. Does the fate of the poorest members of society receive the most consideration, or is it every man for himself? This is a choice that society, voters and politicians will have to make. Additional statistics show, moreover, that more freedom leads to more growth in terms of wealth in general. The greater the increase in overall wealth, the more choices a society will be able to make, and the better off it will be.

Critics will immediately remark that the demonstrably greater wealth and faster growth of the most free societies is unavoidably achieved at the expense of social equality. A society in which the individual has so much freedom to pursue happiness must be – by definition – a less equal society. A dog-eat-dog society in which might makes right and the poor are left to suffer the consequences.

This too appears not to be the case. There is not one single link between a country's economic freedom and the fate of its poor. This is

Illustration 2: **Economic freedom and economic growth* between 1990 and 2010**
Source: Fraser Institute

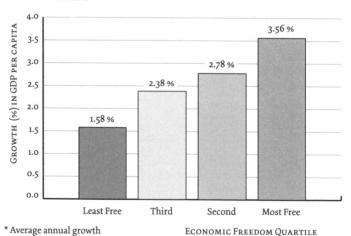

* Average annual growth

evident from illustration 3. Four groups of countries, ranked according to economic freedom, are shown in terms of how much of the national income is earned by the poorest 10% of the population. Although the poorest 10% earn the most numerically in the most free economies, the differences between categories are too small to identify as an actual trend.

As was already apparent above, the limitation of economic freedom has negative consequences for a country: wealth per capita decreases, wealth grows more slowly, and the situation of the poor does not improve in any way.

All cases in which rulers, regimes or governments have tried in the past to restrict the free market have in one way or another ended up failures. In 1959 Communist Party leader Nikita Khrushchev traveled across the United States at the invitation of President Dwight D. Eisenhower, from Harlem to Hollywood. During his travels the leader of the Soviet Union visited a supermarket in San Francisco. He was genuinely moved when he saw how an average housewife

Illustration 3: **Income of the poorest 10% as a percentage of total income**
Source: Fraser Institute

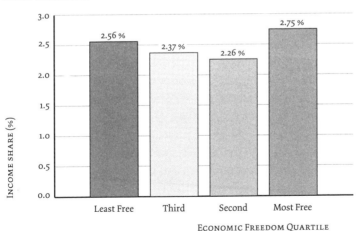

could walk in at any moment of the day and do her shopping, choosing from an assortment of thousands of different products. How different from the Soviet Union, where food shortages, long lines and the black market were the order of the day. Many years later, almost to the very day, another Russian leader, Boris Yeltsin, also visited an American supermarket, this time in Houston. Later, in his autobiography, he would also describe that moment as one of complete shock. In the plane afterwards he was overwhelmed by a great feeling of compassion for the Russian people. A people faced with deprivation and shortages day in, day out because its leaders had such good intentions that they sought to regulate consumer habits and even the very lives of its citizens.

These supermarket experiences must have struck the central planners of the former Soviet Union dumb. How could an average American shopkeeper succeed in offering exactly what all those countless and completely unique consumers were waiting for, while the extremely sophisticated planners of the socialist period only succeeded in offering things for which there was no demand and running out of what was really needed. The only things they could consistently produce in great quantities were long lines and general deprivation.

Why has our trading instinct persisted for millennia and why is the market so successful? Why have experiments with restricting the market always failed in the past? Because no one succeeds in satisfying all those totally different needs of all those thousands, millions and billions of individuals better than the free market.

The importance of free markets can hardly be underestimated. The deep meaning of the free market is, after all, that it enables people to search for ways to improve their own circumstances: of their own accord, without compulsion and sometimes against the will of the religious, moral and political leaders of the moment.

Did the liberation of women in the 1950s happen just like that? Or did it happen because the pharmaceutical industry, by introducing new methods of contraception, satisfied an existing demand? Or did it happen because electrical appliances ensured that household chores took less time, making work outside the home possible? Or perhaps it happened because women muscled their way into the workforce during the war years, thereby proving that they could hold their own in the labor market.

The American civil rights movement also made use of the free market as an instrument for demanding rights and freedoms in the 1950s. The movement began when the black population of Montgomery, Alabama, boycotted segregated buses. Blacks were at that moment second-class citizens, but were finally able to use their power as consumers in a free market as leverage for more political rights as citizens.

Would the Arab Spring have unfolded so easily without social media? Facebook and Twitter were not called into existence by a benevolent government in order to make life easier for its citizens. In the case of Facebook, Mark Zuckerberg had an idea and the necessary freedom to develop it. The deposed leaders of North Africa would never have been willing or able to offer the same freedoms. But the free market penetrates even those areas where it is not allowed to go, offering people a real chance to better their lives.

The frequently desperate ways in which some regimes try to limit the individual choices of citizens or consumers illustrates the power of the free market. The regular attempts at censoring the Internet and social media by the Chinese government, for example, clearly show that a free consumer, and by extension a free citizen, is a threat to a government that seeks to determine what is good for its own population.

People have countless needs: food, drink, shelter and security are the primary human needs. For centuries they were also the only needs people were able to meet. The earliest markets we know of traded in exactly these sorts of products. Where there was demand, supply arose; and where the two met, a market was born. Over the last few centuries the number of human needs has exploded: lighting, heating, transportation, education, healthcare, communication, luxury, culture ... you name it. We cannot conceive of a need so outrageous that there is not someone, somewhere in the world, who can fulfill it.

Today, the 'free market' is often – wrongly – associated with rampant capitalism, exploitation and poverty. Nothing could be further from the truth. The underlying meaning of the 'free market' is that each individual can try to improve his or her own lot. By demanding. By supplying. From the playground to the prisoner-of-war camp. From a supermarket in San Francisco to prehistoric Australia.

In the following chapter we will examine in detail the reasons why the free market is often so controversial, and the arguments used by opponents of the free market. We will then look closely at deviations from the free market. In the first example, we look at government interventions that disturb the workings of the free market; in the second, we look at a dysfunctional free market in which government intervention is necessary.

Two sayings by the Ur-economist Adam Smith (1723-1790) to frame and hang on the wall. More than 200 years after they first saw the light of day, they still describe precisely why we need free markets now more than ever.

"The uniform, constant and uninterrupted effort of every man to better his condition."

People are continually searching for ways to improve their living conditions and have been since the beginning of time. Whether it's about more and better food and drink, security, better health, a longer life, more comfort, a larger or more environmentally friendly house, cultural attractions or better education for our children: we want things to be better. And this is the reason we do business with one another. Because what I want is offered by someone who may be interested in what I have to offer. The inclination to trade is deeply embedded in human nature. War and armed conflicts are perhaps just one constant in human history; our inclination to work together and to conduct trade is another.

Here's an interesting mental exercise for the next time you're traveling or happen to be in a shop or market stall in a distant or not-so-distant country. There are a lot of things you would probably rather not do with that shopkeeper, peddler or merchant. But there is one thing you never even ask yourself about: coming to an agreement about what will be purchased, and for how much. Engaging in trade is so deeply embedded in our genes that we rarely question it, if at all.

"It is not for the benevolence of the butcher, the brewer or the baker that we can expect our dinner, but from their regard to their self-interest."

Charity and compassion do exist. And it's a good thing too. Without compassion and charity the world would be a much darker place.

That we are able to do things for family, acquaintances and perfect strangers, or to give them something for which we expect absolutely nothing in return, makes us human. But this is not what is being described above. It is not out of charity or benevolence that the baker bakes bread, the brewer brews beer or the butcher cuts meat. In the first place they pursue their own enlightened self-interest. But it is precisely because everybody does this that the prosperity of a society can increase to the greatest possible extent. The shopkeeper thinks of her own best interest and tries to better her life. And naturally because she does, she offers her clients the opportunity to do the same.

Does a farmer grow vegetables because he is concerned with the fate of humanity? Does a mechanic repair automobiles out of compassion for the car trouble of his stranded fellow men? Does a chef get up at the crack of dawn and go to the seafood market out of benevolence towards the hungry customers she expects later in the day? No, no and for a third time no! And there is nothing dishonest about this. It is precisely by pursuing their own enlightened self-interest that the farmer, the mechanic and the chef ensure the greatest possibility of wealth for all. And that is Adam Smith's message in a nutshell: the best way to help society as a whole to get ahead is not by allowing a central planning committee to make choices for other individuals out of its own sense of enlightened self-interest. The best way is to let everyone lead their life the way they see fit, to make their own choices and follow their own enlightened self-interest.

CHAPTER 2

Who's afraid of the big, bad free market?

"*The democracy of the market consists in the fact that people themselves make their choices and no dictator has the power to force them to submit to his value judgments.*"
— **Ludwig von Mises**, Austrian economist and philosopher (1881-1973)

The free market is controversial. Those who would be popular in Europe had best turn their backs on the free market. Those who would be hip had better confess to anti-globalist sentiments. Those who talk about the 'dictatorship of the free market' or 'American hypercapitalism' are believed without question. Those who want to be labeled conservative or reactionary, however, had best argue in favor of international free trade. Those who defend the free market are in the best case labeled naïve, in the worst case, proponents of the worldwide exploitation and repression of the poorest people on the planet. Apparently every self-respecting Western intellectual is supposed to be against the free market. The result is that those who defend it are not always considered intellectual.

Criticism of the free market can usually be distilled down to two elementary trains of thought. In the first place there is criticism of the free market as an *ordering mechanism*. The idea that the market – an amalgam of all those people and their desires – should judge the success of a product, service or idea, is unacceptable to many people. The second critique of the free market is largely concerned with its so-called worldwide and dominant character, with all the negative side effects this entails. The free market is identified with exploitation or child labor, and is, moreover, viewed as a disaster for the world's poorest.

THE MARKET VULGARIZES!

The first critique is primarily oriented toward the market as an ordering mechanism. The way in which success, wealth or prosperity comes into being in the free market is usually not based on intellectual, artistic or even social virtues. It is not the person who can express herself most eloquently who becomes rich. Nor is it the best writer. Nor is it the person with the most profound knowledge of western literature. Nor the most intelligent, the most artistic, the most erudite or the best educated. None of the above. Only the person who is best able to estimate what 'the market' needs is going to succeed. Whether it's an improved detergent or a new telephone, cheap plane tickets, a brand of clothing or a kind of beer. The one who can plumb the desires of 'the market' will enjoy success. Better yet: even someone who can hardly read or write can, thanks to the free market, become fabulously wealthy. He who has the best idea at the right moment and can convince the market will reap success. It is, of course, this observation – that financial and business success is determined by popularity – that causes resentment, unrest or open resistance among a number of people.

This is evident from the frequently condescending attitude they show towards people who have become successful thanks to a combination of personal effort and the free market. Succeeding through striving after what 'the market' wants is viewed as pursuing the lowest of human sentiments: greed. Pursuing an artistic or intellectual project is viewed as a tribute to the highest of human sentiments.

That someone can become astronomically rich by designing a new sort of toilet cleaner while a brilliant artist lives in extreme poverty is seen by many intellectuals as a travesty of some kind of natural order. That an engineer can earn many times as much as a philosopher, writer or historian in a free labor market is likewise viewed as an injustice. In a country like France, this attitude has become second nature. Almost the entire intellectual elite of that country rejects 'the free market' or 'capitalism'. Apparently they are of the opinion that the engines that drive social success are insufficiently uplifting.

By elevating popularity to a measure of success, the free market – according to many intellectuals, at least – encourages the 'Disney-fication,' 'McDonaldization' or 'Facebookization' of society: a world in which all culture will be reduced to one big revolting mush, in which the most popular common denominator is elevated to the norm. The core idea behind this world vision can be summarized in a few words: an immense disdain for the free choice of each citizen. A disdain for those who watch commercial television of their own volition, who book a package tour to a popular destination, who go to McDonald's, or who like to go to the movies and see American blockbusters. A disdain for the free choice of each citizen, because together their collective choice supposedly undermines 'high culture'.

Everyone is free to make his or her own choices. Whether he likes to drink French wine or a Thai-Austrian energy drink. Whether she goes to the movies to see French art-house films or American blockbusters. Whether he likes to listen to sentimental Flemish tunes, French techno or American hip-hop. The free market is an aid that enables people to make better choices of their own. Perhaps some people are horrified at the idea that an average Indian or Chinese will soon be able to go shopping at the British supermarket chain Tesco, buy furniture at the Swedish Ikea, drive around in a German car and drink African coffee in an American Starbucks. That's just the way it is. Every citizen has the right to make his or her own choices. At the same time, no one has the right to present his choices as better, morally superior or more authentic than those of someone else – let alone impose his own choice or own culture on someone else. Individual preferences and social cultures are constantly in motion. Those who want to protect their own culture completely against the free market and the allegedly corrupt foreign or leveling influences it brings with it should probably start a folklore museum.

THE DICTATORSHIP OF THE FREE MARKET!

The second objection of self-declared intellectuals is that the free market is particularly bad for the world's poorest citizens. It gives their inherent rejection of the free market a practical, humanitarian spin: "You see, we reject the free market because it is disastrous for the poor ..." Developing countries, in their opinion, are heavily burdened by the 'dictatorship of the free market', and for this same reason the lives of the poorest are completely torn apart by this same free market. There is hardly an assertion that could be further from the truth. Inhabitants of developing countries are, more often than we imagine, victims of the complete absence of free markets. The poorest people in the world usually live in circumstances in which they have anything but the freedom to shape their own lives: neither to come and go as they please, nor to buy or sell what they want.

The self-immolation of Tunesian grocer Mohamed Bouazizi is generally seen as the start of the Arab Spring. Bouazizi lost his father when he was three years old. When his stepfather fell ill, he dropped out of school and began selling fruit and vegetables from a stall in order to support his family. Every day he was confronted with bureaucrats or police to whom he had to pay *baksheesh*. It was when he could no longer afford to pay these bribes, and agents came to confiscate his stall that he set himself on fire in utter despair. It was a total lack of freedom and free markets that drove him to despair. Bouazizi was only looking for what the American president Thomas Jefferson once described as "Life, liberty and the pursuit of happiness ..." And of course, this was what a corrupt system prevented him from doing. In Egypt – that other exemplary land of the Arab Spring – the pattern is comparable: scarcely any freedom, scarcely any free market. For an average Egyptian, it is nearly impossible to get a job without connections or bribes to someone in the government. Offering one's labor in a free market where only skills and talent count: impossible. Beginning a business of one's own: almost impossible without kickbacks. A driver's license: pay up. Enforcing a contract before a judge: only if you know someone in the regime.

Those who curtail the free market, curtail freedom. That is why there are virtually no free markets in dictatorial regimes, whether North Korea, Congo, Cuba or the former East Germany. A regime that does not trust its populace with exercising its freedom of choice in the voting booth every couple of years will certainly not allow that populace to make its own choices on the free market on a daily basis.

It is all too easily forgotten that the free market – certainly for the world's poorest – is often a very good thing. Not only does the free market give them the chance to offer their labor, services or products to a much larger public, as consumers they also have much greater access to goods and services, often at prices they can actually afford.

Thanks to competition and the free market, most poor people worldwide spend less of their income on food today than they did a 100, 50 or even 20 years ago. In those developing countries that decided to opt for the free market and opened their borders to imported goods, the population has a much greater choice of products at lower prices. To give but one example, foreign supermarkets were not allowed in India until 2011. Under pressure from the lobby of local merchants and shopkeepers, major international chains such as Walmart, Tesco and Carrefour were kept out for years. Thanks to their efforts, millions of impoverished Indians paid far too much for far too few products that were often substandard to boot. In the meantime the Indian government has relaxed this prohibition, albeit reluctantly and not entirely.

CHILD LABOR!

Crusaders against the free market have one last and extremely emotional line of defense at their disposal: child labor! Because doesn't the globalized free market ensure that children – often young children – will be dehumanized, turned into production factors and forced to do dangerous, unhealthy work? Shouldn't we organize a boycott against countries where child labor still exists? No, no and no!

Let me be very clear: child labor and child exploitation are shameful. Children should be able to play, go to school and grow up in a safe environment. On this everyone agrees. For many children in the world, however, this is unfortunately not the case. But this has nothing to do with the free market. On the contrary.

To this day, many people associate this with children working long hours in factories. These children risked their health and often their lives. Child labor is perhaps also in the collective memory of the industrial revolution that speaks most vividly to the imagination. Nor is this unique to Flanders or Belgium: in other Western countries child labor is likewise associated with that period in our history. Nevertheless, the industrial revolution did not mark the beginning of child labor. It marked the beginning of the end of child labor.

By equating the industrial revolution with child labor, some assume that the period before was better. They pay homage to an idyllic image of pastoral life in the country. An idyllic countryside without belching smokestacks, factory gates or noisy machines, where children could play all day. Very idyllic indeed: child mortality hovered around 50%, disease, infections, hunger, poor living conditions in thatched huts and a hard life working the land, for children too – especially children. The start of the industrial revolution was the very first time in history that people – especially those who were not from nobility – could improve their own lot. Why did the factories find so many employees in the 19th century who were willing to move to the city in order to find work in those factories? Because life in the country was so much better and more idyllic? The industrial revolution meant the end of child labor. It was the mechanization of agriculture and industry that finally hastened the end of low-productivity child labor.

Child labor did not disappear thanks to a legal prohibition, but rather thanks to technological progress and increasing prosperity. It is exactly the same way that child labor will disappear from the rest of the planet. Parents in developing countries who send their children out to work do not do so in order to punish their children. They do it because their children's income is necessary for the family's survival. It is an illusion, however, to think that child labor in developing countries will disappear simply by prohibiting it or by boycotting countries where child labor still exists. Most child labor in developing countries does not take place in sectors that are visible to the average Westerner. Most child labor is not found in the workshops where shorts, skirts, or toy components are assembled for Western consumers. Most children who work do so in agriculture, construction, or worse: as house slaves or child prostitutes. Forbidding child labor in the clothing industry – which is visible to the West – will only cause children in the clothing workshops to migrate to those sectors that are invisible to the West. But the Western consumer could not care less. His conscience is appeased with a label that says his sweater, shorts or shirt was not made by children's hands. What those same children's hands may have been forced to do in order to make a living does not interest him.

The best way to eliminate child labor is to ensure that developing countries are more prosperous. This will only happen if there is more economic growth and more free markets. A boycott against countries where child labor still exists will slow down growth, increase family poverty and work counterproductively. It is only when families can make progress and earn sufficient income that child labor will no longer be necessary to make ends meet.

Just as the industrial revolution did in the West, technological progress today will help put an end to child labor. A farmer in the southern hemisphere who can only work his fields by hand needs all the hands he can get. Even if they are children's hands. When he has a tractor or other farming equipment, his productivity will increase by leaps and bounds. In comparison to the tractor or farming equipment, a child working in the field scarcely produces any surplus value. From then on, raising the family income is better achieved by sending the child to school than by letting him work the land. So that sooner or later he will be able to operate or repair a tractor or piece of farming equipment himself. So that he can read and understand the instructions for tools, fertilizers or seeds. Western activists who reject products from the southern hemisphere because of their high CO_2 footprint, child labor or poor working conditions deny the poorest producers in the world access to the wealthiest consumers in the world. This is the best way to ensure the continuation of low incomes, low productivity and child labor. Only through more free market and more free trade can the poorest populations in the world get access to the wealthiest populations in the world. That is their only ticket to prosperity. A trade boycott is a round-trip ticket to misery.

THE FREE MARKET IS AN OPINION POLL

The free market is a giant opinion poll. Every day, every hour, every minute and every second, the opinions of thousands, millions and billions of consumers and producers come together. Without filling in any forms, without having to pick up the phone and without having to take any multiple-choice tests, they all give their opinion. Do they prefer tea or coffee? Nespresso or filtered coffee? Would they rather watch a film on their computer, on TV or in a movie theater? Do they like to spend their vacations on the beach or in Provence? How much more are they prepared to pay for a Bruce Springsteen concert than a concert by Slayer? Would they rather watch football or go to a museum? Do they find it more interesting to travel by train than by plane? What sort of books do they prefer to read?

There is no better, more massive, more permanent and more efficient opinion poll than the free market. Let the same citizen actually fill in questionnaires about coffee, tea, Provence, Bruce Springsteen or their favorite film and the results will be much less reliable. In the first place, the administration of this type of written opinion poll is unimaginably complex, laborious and time-consuming. The moment the results are made known, they are already obsolete. Moreover, it is questionable whether opinion polls on paper are more reliable than the free market. That is, it represents the difference between a *stated preference* and a *revealed preference.* In other words, someone can make out on paper that he or she really cares about the environment, is unsatisfied with his or her job, likes to buy bio foodstuffs or only swears by brand-name coffee, but the only real proof is what he or she does in a free-market context. Of course, this necessitates a market that is completely free – a market in which no one is forced to participate, to buy or to sell. An environment in which no one is obliged to act and everyone acts in order to be better off.

Every transaction expresses the actual preference of the consumer. At various times throughout the day, everyone knows what he or she thinks and how he or she feels. Whether faced with a flea market, a supermarket, a stock market or a labor market: it is a concatenation of free choices. Each and every day, people make thousands, millions and billions of such choices. Although it would be near impossible to keep track of who made what choice and why, the final results of these choices can be clearly deciphered: the quantity of beer purchased on a warm Friday evening, the most popular vegetable in the first week of July, the most frequently downloaded number on iTunes, the number of people looking for a new job through a temp agency, the best-selling book, the average price of a hotel room during the weekend as opposed to weekdays, the fact as to whether a child in Bangladesh goes to school until the age of 10 or 15, whether a farmer will invest in a new piece of equipment, how much prices have to be reduced in order to sell all the clothing left in the store, the price difference between a coffee at the Starbucks in Antwerp and the one in New York, between an apartment in Brussels and one in Manhattan... Anything desirable, popular or scarce will increase in price. Anything undesirable, unpopular or plentiful will decrease in price – whether it's a telephone, a house in Provence, an employee with an engineering diploma or an apartment in Manhattan.

The evolution of all those quantities and prices is the most detailed picture of how free, unconstrained citizens in the world see things. No one is obliged to buy a CD by Bruce Springsteen. No one is obliged to drink soft drinks instead of water. No one is obliged to vacation at the coast instead of Provence. No one is obliged to pay high prices for a popular concert with a limited number of seats. In a free market, free citizens make their own decisions without anyone passing judgment on it. That is also the ultimate meaning of the free market: it is *the* place where free and independent citizens are constantly asked for their opinion and where they may constantly express that opinion through their behavior. Whether they are rich or poor, black or white, young or old, man or woman. The free market is the ultimate combination of individual freedom and freedom of expression. But on a *very* large scale. The conclusion is also crystal clear: those who do not believe in the free market, do not believe in freedom.

CHAPTER 3

Good intentions, unintentional consequences

"The road to hell is paved with good intentions."
– popular saying

"The more the state plans, the more difficult planning becomes for the individual." **– Friedrich Hayek**, Austrian economist and political philosopher, Nobel Prize winner in economics (1899-1992)

The year 1585 stands recorded in the history of the Low Countries as a very bad year. The Spanish took over Antwerp and blockaded the Scheldt – a blockade that would last for centuries. The heyday of the once flourishing metropolis was over, and the economic and financial center of the Low Countries would subsequently shift to Amsterdam. The end of Antwerp's golden 16th century heralded the beginning of Amsterdam's golden seventeenth. A little-known footnote from this historical episode is that the former city council of Antwerp was in part responsible for this state of affairs, thanks to its intervention in the market...

From the year 1584, Spanish troops – under the Duke of Parma – already had the city of Antwerp surrounded. The city was under siege, but the river Scheldt was not yet completely blockaded. Antwerp could still secure victuals and other necessary resources by ship, although it had become riskier and more difficult than before for the merchants willing to undertake this enterprise. Greater risks lead to an increase in the price of all manner of foodstuffs. Concerned, the city council wanted to pay for the cost of living by enacting maximum prices. Paradoxically enough, these good intentions seem to have dealt the besieged city a fatal blow. The imposition of maximum prices caused the transport of victuals to dry up almost overnight. Merchants from outside the city had to risk their own lives and brave Spanish artillery for a price that was scarcely higher than what they could get for their grain, meat and vegetables in less dangerous marketplaces. On the other hand, the prices were artificially held in check so that the inhabitants of Antwerp had no way of knowing that food was becoming scarce. They continued to consume as before so that the city ran through its existing provisions in no time at all. Antwerp's decision to introduce maximum prices appears to have been an even more effective strategy for starving the city than the Duke of Parma's siege itself.

It is abundantly clear that the introduction of maximum prices encouraged and even caused scarcity rather than eliminating it. This is clear from illustration 4, which describes the situation in 1585.

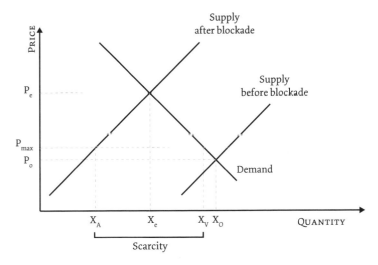

The demand for victuals is given by the demand curve. The vertical axis represents prices; the horizontal axis represents the available amount of food. The higher the price, the lower the quantity in demand and vice versa. The supply curve at the lower right shows the price charged by suppliers of victuals before the blockade. Transporting food was relatively simple, hence a large quantity of food X_0 was offered at a relatively low price P_0. Because of the blockade, it became far more expensive and increasingly risky to transport goods, so the demand curve shifts towards the upper left. For the same quantity, merchants now get a much higher price. Because the merchants must evade the Duke of Parma's artillery, they ask a much higher price than before the blockade. One of the consequences of the blockade was that the quantity of food available would drop drastically and the price would increase sharply: the new equilibrium price was eventually P_e and the equilibrium quantity X_e.

In order to address the popular protest against the rising cost of living, the city council decided to introduce a maximum price P_{max}. The consequences were double. In the first place, the public did not feel the need to decrease its consumption in any way. The price remained low and so they could demand quantity X_V. This was a quantity that suppliers would never consider offering at that price. For the maximum price, they were only prepared to offer quantity X_A, much less than they would have offered had the market remained free.

The result of the measure is clear: consumers were encouraged to consume more; producers were discouraged to offer more. The result was great scarcity. Precisely the opposite of what the city council hoped to accomplish with its maximum prices.

The government imposes maximum prices because it hopes, in this way, to make itself popular among the governed. They can point to the merchants who take advantage of the situation by profiting from price increases at the expense of the consumer. By proclaiming maximum prices they appear to be taking a jab at the merchants. In the end, however, they are shooting themselves – and the consumers – in the foot. A maximum price may make life easier for the consumer in the short term, but over the long term the supply side is destroyed.

A splendid illustration of this problem is given by Nobel Prize winner Paul Samuelson in the sixth and seventh editions of his handbook on economics. He describes a medieval Flanders in which famine is the order of the day and in which there are two imaginary kingdoms: Zig and Zog...

In the kingdom of Zig, King Jan ordered all farmers to bring their harvest to the city. He paid them a fair price for their grain and rationed the food supply for the whole population. The famine continued, and although people were dying in great numbers, they praised the king for his justness.

In Zog, the merchants had filled their silos to the brim with grain during the years of bountiful harvests. When famine struck after the crops failed, they quickly doubled their prices and made money hand over fist. Business was going so well that merchants from Zog went looking for grain in other regions so that they could sell it at home.

Moreover, other merchants and farmers came from far and wide to provide Zog with grain. Farmers from Zig even sold their grain to merchants from Zog, because they could turn a better profit that way. The longer the famine persisted, the higher the prices. When it was over, nearly all the inhabitants of Zog owed money to the grain merchants, but they had survived. The grain merchants had become fabulously rich thanks to the period of scarcity. But by importing extra grain themselves, they avoided additional price increases. The supply increased: therefore the price did not increase much more. The merchants of Zog had increased their fortunes fourfold, but without competition from farmers and other merchants from outside the kingdom, they could have easily increased their wealth 20 times over.

PRICE AS A SIGNAL

In chapter 1 we saw that engaging in trade is deeply embedded in human nature. Governments do not impose trade with one another or the creation of markets; these things come about naturally. Nor are prices imposed, decreed or chiseled in stone tablets. They are the result of interaction between supply and demand. In this way, prices always signal the relative scarcity of goods and services. When the price of ice cream rises in the summer, the rising price will encourage producers to produce more. Sometimes this goes quickly and it is simply a question of allowing production facilities to operate for longer hours. Sometimes new investments have to be made first or new employees hired before supplies can be increased. But for the suppliers, price is always a signal to which they will respond. Higher prices encourage production and supply; low prices have the opposite effect.

Price is also important as a signal for consumers. A high price will discourage the consumer from buying and cause a change of behavior; a low price will stimulate him to buy. If the price of coffee increases sharply, for example, the consumer will start drinking less coffee or switch over to alternatives like tea.

The market price is also a complex interaction between various elements. Fluctuations in supply and demand, changing production techniques, climatological effects, seasons, fashions, or consumer preferences can all play a role. Still, the entire complex chain of interactions is reflected in one market price. The one-sided imposition of a maximum price sends conflicting signals to consumers and producers alike. Consumers receive the signal that they may continue to consume as before – after all, the price has a ceiling. Producers, by contrast, receive the message that they had better supply less. The combination of the two ensures that there will be an imbalance between supply and demand.

Maximum prices arise out of good intentions, but lead to perverse effects precisely because they discourage the market suppliers from offering more. When prices increase because of failed crops or a supply that is far too small, that sends two signals. In the first place it will encourage the consumer to be more careful with what they have. In the second place, the high prices will attract new suppliers. In this way, the supply increases and there will be downward pressure on the prices. In the long run, markets always find new equilibrium. A price that is 'unacceptably' high or low is therefore a contradiction in terms. The activities of producers and consumers lead to an equilibrium price. A maximum price seems to be a solution for shortages on the market, but this is not the case. A maximum price is never a sustainable solution; it is a short-term way to combat symptoms.

HURRICANES AND METALLICA

One intervention in market forces in Belgium that immediately comes to mind is the prohibition on reselling concert tickets at a profit. In practice this also counts as imposing a maximum price. A short while ago, I bought a ticket to a Metallica concert in Belgium for around €100. Owing to circumstances, I was not able to attend, so I had to dispose of my ticket. The concert was so popular that I could get many times the original €100 for the ticket on eBay. In the end I did not sell the ticket on the free market, but to a friend, for the original purchase price.

In this example it is not about choosing between selling to a friend or a stranger, or about selling at a friendly price or at the market price. It is about the fact that the law obliges everyone to sell his ticket to a stranger at a friendly price. When there are many more prospective buyers than available tickets, then we have a shortage of supply. Imagine that there are 20,000 available tickets and ten times as many candidates who want to attend the concert. If the tickets were auctioned to the highest bidder, the final price per ticket would probably be much higher – perhaps even as much as €300 or even €400 per ticket. But for that price there would be just as many tickets as prospective buyers.

A frequently heard argument is that, in this way, only the most affluent would be able to find their way to the concert. This reasoning is false for two reasons. First, there are many affluent people who would never want to go to a Metallica concert, not even if the tickets were free. Willingness to pay has nothing to do with monthly income. Some people would spend a lot of money to go to a Metallica concert, but would never pay a dime to see Bruce Springsteen, while others only want to hear Wagner from a plush velvet seat in an opera house.

Second, the selection mechanism 'willingness to pay' is replaced by another, completely arbitrary mechanism when we are dealing with maximum prices. As we saw earlier, the free market is the best way to unite the desires of producers and consumers. Because the tickets may no longer be sold to the highest bidder, the price no longer determines who can go and who cannot. Imagine that I didn't sell my Metallica ticket to a friend, but that I had offered it on eBay for the original price of €100. Accordingly, I would get dozens, if not hundreds of candidate concertgoers. How would I decide who gets my ticket? I only have one ticket and there are hundreds of metalheads who want it. Do I have to organize a lottery and allow statistics and chance to decide the fate of my ticket? But that's not fair to the person who reacted most quickly to my advertisement. Should I perhaps sell it to the first potential buyer who reacts? But that wouldn't be fair to those who don't have time to sit glued to their computers 24 hours a day. Should I sell it to the person who can write the most touching or convincing reason why he or she wants to see Metallica? But that's not being fair to people who have no talent for writing. Or should I sell it to the person who can stand on their head the longest? Or kick a football the farthest? Or who knows the most digits of pi by heart? In short, if you limit the free market and price as a selection mechanism, you have to find some other arbitrary way of distributing scarce goods among many interested parties. The chance of getting a ticket in one of those 'other ways' is anything but fairly distributed.

Another striking example of this problem played out when hurricane Katrina swept through the United States in 2005. This country is affected every year by heavy storms, which also means that there is a massive exodus of people in the expected path of each new hurricane. The enormous line of cars naturally needs a huge supply of gasoline, in response to which gas station owners raise their prices at such moments. Every year this leads to heated discussions and some politicians and judges promise they will restrict such practices, if not put an end to them. They lament the 'unreasonable' prices that are asked of people fleeing from the violence of nature. Gas station owners are depicted as profiteers, while they are only reacting to altered circumstances.

The equilibrium price that comes about is always the result of supply *and* demand. Both parties are thus responsible for the price. A gas station owner who is confronted with a long line of cars instead of a couple of cars per hour will raise his prices. His supply of fuel is, after all, limited. It goes against any form of logic to expect a gas station owner in this situation to charge a 'reasonable' price. The definition of 'reasonable' will, moreover, be different for everyone.

Imagine that the government imposes a maximum price of $2 per gallon for gasoline – the pre-Katrina price – in order to prevent such gas station owners/profiteers from raising their prices. The result is that those fleeing the hurricane will not be forced in any way to limit their demand. At $5 per gallon, everyone might have filled his tank halfway – not all the way, but enough to reach safer ground. At an artificial price of $2 per gallon, the first customers to reach the station will fill their tanks to the limit and maybe a couple of jerry cans as well. The fact that as a result of their actions, nothing will be left for those who fled later, and that these people will arrive to find nothing but closed gas stations be the first to get stranded on the way out of town, won't mean a thing to the customers who got there first. Although they are introduced with the opposite intention, maximum prices always help scarcity along.

Imposing maximum prices is always undertaken with noble intentions: keeping products affordable for everyone and avoiding exploitation. The problem is that it gives the short-term consumer interests one-sided precedence over those of the producers.

MINIMUM WAGES: DIFFERENT TARGET, SAME PROBLEM

We just saw that the government imposes maximum prices in an attempt to protect consumers. Sometimes they will also attempt to do the opposite by introducing minimum prices. The problem, however, is exactly the same. Maximum prices encourage consumption, but at the same time, discourage production. As a result, a shortage arises: precisely the opposite of what the government had in mind. With minimum prices, part of the market is also ignored. Minimum prices primarily benefit suppliers, while the demand side gets lost in the shuffle.

Minimum wages are the most striking example of this phenomenon. These are effectively minimum prices that are introduced on the labor market: the suppliers of labor are potential employees; the demanders are the employers. Here too the government usually has noble motives. For one reason or another, they find the existing wages in certain sectors too low for a dignified human existence and introduce a minimum wage, or raise the existing minimum wage. When that minimum wage climbs above market equilibrium, however, it leads to perverse effects. Higher minimum wages have always had the opposite effect on the suppliers (employees) and consumers (employers) of labor. With the introduction of a minimum wage above market equilibrium, more employees will compete for existing jobs. For employers, the opposite is true: if wages are higher, they will want to offer fewer jobs. The result of the higher minimum wage will not offer better protection to the least skilled workers. On the contrary, the direct result for them will be higher unemployment. This is shown clearly in illustration 5 below. The minimum wage is higher than the wage on the free market. As a result, the readiness of em-

Illustration 5: **Good intentions that lead to unemployment**

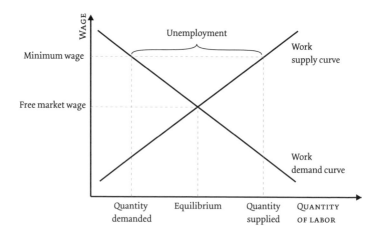

ployers to hire new employees decreases, while the readiness of employees to seek employment rises at the same time. The result is involuntary unemployment.

Let us be clear: concern for bettering the lot of the weakest members of society is in itself laudable; it is an essential part of a civilized society. People who work for the lowest wages are, after all, the most vulnerable members of society. However, there are much more effective ways of helping them along than simply intervening in price mechanisms. Direct income assistance, for example, is one way to help improve the circumstances of the weakest members of society. The best way, however, is still education, training or instruction. This is the best guarantee of higher productivity, a high surplus value and thus higher wages. The imposition of a higher minimum wage is anything but sustainable.

While higher minimum wages attract more people to low-paying jobs on the one hand, employers, on the other, will be less inclined to employ more people at those higher wages. Like maximum prices, the imposition of higher minimum wages is a measure that costs the government nothing in the short term. The costs are apparently born by the employers, who will have to pay more for unskilled labor. In reality, however, it will actually be the unskilled workers themselves who pay the toll in the form of reduced opportunities on the job market and higher unemployment.

A wage – like any other price – does not just appear out of nowhere. An employer is motivated by how much a given employee can contribute to the company's results. This is also the upper limit of how much he can afford to pay in wages. A minimum wage that exceeds the capacities or productivity of an unskilled worker is thus an implicit prohibition against exercising a profession that sentences that unskilled worker to unemployment.

The success of domestic help via service vouchers in Belgium today shows abundantly that price is always a signal. With the previous official minimum price for domestic help, a thriving black market sprang into existence: the demand for officially sanctioned labor was many times smaller than the supply. The price of the 'official' labor was so high that the demanders of domestic help were not prepared to pay the official price. The previous 'minimum price' for official labor was thus far above the market equilibrium price. The introduction of service vouchers amounts to nothing less than the reduction of the official minimum wage for unskilled labor to something in the neighborhood of the market equilibrium. The overwhelming success of this program today also shows that a lower entry threshold in the labor market does indeed counteract unemployment and illegal work. The previous – higher – minimum wage for domestic help was effectively a tax on unskilled labor, which pushed many of the weaker members of society in the direction of jobs in the illegal circuit or even unemployment. In fact, it amounted to a prohibition against pursuing a profession for unskilled workers in legal jobs. However well intentioned and noble it may have been, a higher minimum wage did not improve the lot of the least skilled workers. On the contrary, it threatened to push them out of the market altogether and into illegal work or unemployment.

GOOD INTENTIONS, GOOD SOLUTION

If a higher minimum wage does not help improve the lot of the weakest members of society, what could the solution be? It cannot possibly be the idea to drive people with few skills or education into permanent poverty. One possible solution is known as the earned income tax credit. The lowest bracket of the income tax is currently untaxed. One could go a step further and decide to assign the lowest bracket a negative income tax rate – but only on the condition that the money was earned in an official paying job. This effectively amounts to a wage subsidy in addition to net earnings. In this way, we kill two birds with one stone. For the least educated, the difference between a monthly welfare allowance and wages from paid work becomes much greater. Hence, the stimulus to go out and find paying work is much greater. What they keep from their earnings is – thanks to the negative tax, which is effectively a wage subsidy – much greater than what an employer pays for their net wages. For the employer, the lowest gross wage does not increase. Hence, he will not reduce his demand for labor.

The second and most important solution for the least skilled members of society is ... schooling. Education, schooling, life skills and permanent instruction are the best ways to earn a higher wage. Not the arbitrary imposition of higher wages, but the acquisition of skills that justify a higher wage. Through more skills, additional training or more work experience, an employee will become increasingly attractive to potential employers. The latter will also be prepared to pay increasingly higher wages for the labor of the employee in question. More training, more and better skills are the only way to help the weakest members of society in a sustainable way.

For both minimum prices and maximum prices the same verdict applies: good intentions can lead to unintended, harmful consequences. Imposing an arbitrary price denies the existence of a market – a market with countless demanders and suppliers, each with their own individual motives. An arbitrary price denies demanders and suppliers and distorts their incentives. Moreover, interventions in market forces lead to perverse effects and result in the reduction of wealth. Still, not all government interventions in the market are undesirable. On the contrary: in the next chapter we will see that under certain circumstances, government intervention is not only desirable, but also indispensable.

While I was studying at university, I worked in a fast-food restaurant for a little over a year. Between 15 and 20 hours per weekend, at various hours of the day, and in various functions. You could call it a 'hamburger job'. Obviously I met very few highly educated people there, at least not on my side of the cash register, where I was most often stationed.

My colleagues were a colorful mix of students on the one hand and unskilled youth on the other. It was hard work, not exactly glamorous and you would never get rich doing it. But precisely because the wages were not high – not for the employees so certainly not for the employer who had to pay them – pretty much anyone could have the chance to start working there. Anyone who could read, write, count and who asked, could start working. The low wages set a very low standard and obliged the employer not to be too selective when hiring. Everyone got a chance. The denigrating way some people talk about 'hamburger jobs' goes too far.

What people often forget is the way that these low threshold jobs give people the chance to enter the labor market. Every job is, after all, an opportunity to learn. For many it may seem obvious, but there are many, many people who did not always get the right life skills in their upbringing or education. Finishing an assignment on time, honoring agreements, getting out of bed on time, listening to a boss, combining work and leisure time, improvising, learning new things, following guidelines, handling large amounts of money, customer friendliness, conflict management... These are invalua-

© istockphoto.com

ble skills that you don't learn while unemployed – unemployed, because a too high minimum wage has priced you out of the job market.

Moreover, not one of the people with whom I worked back then still works there today. Precisely because the low threshold offered them a step up to a job in which they could learn and grow and move on to more and better things. It is also up to individuals themselves to take additional steps to improve their situation – by learning additional skills, moving up in their chosen profession and pursuing additional education. Exactly as Adam Smith would have wanted them to.

CHAPTER 4

In search of the missing market

"In general, industrialists are interested, not in the social, but only in the private, net product of their operations."
— **Arthur Cecil Pigou**, English economist (1877-1959), specialized in welfare economics

"You never miss the water till the well runs dry."
— **English saying**

"Without property rights, no other rights are possible."
— **Ayn Rand**, American novelist and philosopher (1905-1982)

The ocean does not belong to anyone. By extension, the fish in the ocean do not belong to anyone either. While they are swimming out there, they do not provide anyone – except perhaps divers, documentary makers or underwater biologists – with an economic surplus value. They only do that once they have landed on the deck of a fishing boat. Only when the fish has been caught and is dead, can it be sold. In other words: for a fisherman, the only valuable fish is a dead fish. It does not require a lot of imagination to see that this logic quickly leads to overfishing. Each fisherman, motivated by his own self-interest, will try to catch as many fish possible – preferably before his competitors can do the same.

Each fisherman will realize sooner or later that collective fishing behavior leads to overfishing and that his own livelihood will eventually be at stake. But one individual fisherman alone cannot make a difference. Imagine now that he is concerned with the consequences of overfishing for his own income in the long run. And then imagine that he will, for this reason, fish less for the time being. It probably wouldn't make much difference. On the contrary, other fishermen would take advantage of the reduction in competition in order to be able to catch more themselves. The core of the problem is also clear: each individual fisherman sees 100% of the profits that come from the fish he catches. He does not really feel responsible for damage to the communal fishing grounds by overfishing or even the extinction of fish species in the area.

The California biologist Garrett Hardin was the first to describe this kind of problem in the scientific magazine *Science*, in an article entitled *The Tragedy of the Commons*. In the original article from 1968, he describes how many communities, villages or towns in medieval Europe had a communal field, the commons. Each farmer had the right to let his own sheep or cows graze there. The more animals could graze, the more wool, milk or meat they provided the farmer. More grazing meant more profit. At the same time, each grazing animal limited the supply of grass available to other animals. In extreme cases, there was a risk of overgrazing.

Hardin showed that in such a system, each farmer had every interest in allowing his own animals to graze as much as possible on the commons, and as little as possible in his own field. If the sheep or cows only grazed on his own land, the farmer would have to take into account not only the profits (milk, wool, meat), but also the costs (overgrazing). In the case of the commons he didn't have to do that: his profits – meat, milk and wool – were privatized; the cost – overgrazing – was socialized.

One last example from our own time, and very close to home: the communal kitchen in a house full of students. This is often the dirtiest and least maintained spot in the whole house. When one housemate leaves behind a mess, why shouldn't the rest do likewise? Everyone is responsible for his own room, but the kitchen is the responsibility of all the residents. For this reason, no one feels responsible for it individually, unless the residents agree in advance how best to handle the situation. And these are the kind of agreements that can offer a way out of this important failure of the free market. The cause of the tragedy is simply a lack of property rights. Or more specifically: poorly regulated property rights lead to negative social results.

SELF-INTEREST DOESN'T ALWAYS WORK

In the first chapter we saw that after a business transaction, both parties were happier and more satisfied than before. Trade and the interaction between supply and demand on the free market should, in this way, always ensure a better, happier society. This is how Adam Smith saw things in his *Wealth of Nations*: when everyone devotes his own labor and industry to his own self-interest, society as a whole will benefit. *"By directing that industry in such a manner as its produce may be of greatest value, he intends only his own gain, and he is in this, as in many other cases, led by an invisible hand to promote an end which was no part of his intention."*

Why, then, doesn't self-interest work for the fishermen, the commons, or the kitchen in the student house? The way the free market is supposed to work implicitly assumes that property rights are well defined. In that case, each transaction will contribute to the common good. Those who think only of their own profits but let others pay the price do not contribute to the common good. Just as someone who steals a bicycle and then sells it to someone else does not make a positive contribution to the wealth of society as a whole.

These types of problems are generally classed together under the rubric of externalities. These are situations in which the behavior of consumers or producers has negative consequences for others, and in which the producers do not take the latter into account – or do not consider them sufficiently. In this case we refer to them as negative externalities. A chemical factory will only take into account its own costs for personnel, technical facilities, raw materials and energy when calculating costs and setting prices. As a result, it will take little or no account of emissions, environmental risks or inconvenience to those who live in the neighborhood. A nightclub in a residential area will only take into account its costs and profits at the end of the day, while neglecting the consequences of excessive noise and traffic for those in the neighborhood. An individual driver takes into account only his own driving time and comfort, but does not consider sufficiently the consequences for the environment, surrounding residents, or other drivers (see the box "Clearances on the highway"). Even the financial crisis of a few years ago is a typical example of externalities. A financial institution will in the first place consider its own costs and profits, but will take insufficient account of the consequences of its choices for the entire financial system or the entire economy.

In all of the cases just mentioned, we are confronted with negative externalities: the producer estimates his private costs as lower than the actual social costs. The result: society as a whole receives more damage and annoyance than it would like to deal with. More waste, noise, financial risk and environmental pollution than society wants or needs.

In illustration 7 the problem is summed up schematically. The vertical axis shows various possible tuna prices; the horizontal axis shows tuna supplies. The rising curve MPC is the tuna supply curve. The lower the price, the smaller the supply and vice versa. The demand curve MSB runs in the opposite direction: the higher the price, the less the demand. We subsequently observe that equilibrium arises. At a quantity Q_1 and a price P_1 supply and demand are in perfect equilibrium. Q_1 is the equilibrium quantity, P_1 the equilibrium price.

Time to add the 'tragedy of the commons' to the mix. We know in the meantime that each fisherman only takes his own profits and costs into account. The latter are represented by the curve MPC. Each individual fisherman forgets, however, to take into account the costs he generates for all the other fishermen: the cost of overfishing and even the extinction of certain species. The curve MSC also depicts

Illustration 7: **Whose tuna is it anyway: yours, mine or ours?**

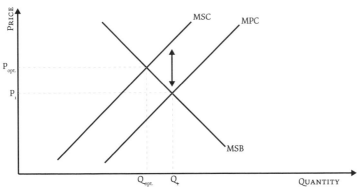

MPC = Marginal Private Costs   Q opt. = Socially Optimal Quantity
MSC = Marginal Social Costs   P opt. = Socially Optimal Price
MSB = Marginal Social Benefits

the actual costs to society. In this case they are clearly higher than the individual costs per fisherman. When each individual fisherman takes only his own boat and his own catch into consideration, he structurally underestimates the actual costs. The result: much more damage will be done than socially desirable. In total, a quantity Q_1 is caught, which is higher than socially desirable. The reason for this is that the fishermen only take their own interests into account and not those of society. The conclusion is clear: the sum of all the individual choices made by producers and consumers no longer leads to a socially optimal outcome. This also seems to go directly against Adam Smith's assertion that society as a whole always makes the most progress when everyone looks after his or her best interests.

The assumption that enlightened self-interest always leads to social improvement is clearly not supported here. Each tuna fisherman chooses in favor of his own self-interest by catching as much tuna possible. The same can be said about the number of cows on the commons, the number of environmental risks associated with the chemical plant, the financial risks taken by banks, the noise pollution caused by a nightclub or the traffic jams created by excess automobile traffic.

What is the conclusion? Should all harmful results be banned entirely? Do CO_2 emissions have to be reduced to zero and excess noise made illegal? Certainly not: that would mean every activity that had an impact on others would have to be stopped. The solution consists effectively in having the one causing the damage to take the total social costs into account. When that happens, the socially desired equilibrium will come about. Less will be produced (Q_{opt}) and production will be sold at a higher price (P_{opt}).

In case it has not become clear in the meantime: for today's environmentalists, the 'tragedy of the commons' is pretty much the only economic cornerstone of their worldview and ideology. The story captures most of their policy points perfectly: individuals do not take the consequences of their behavior for the community into account – or not sufficiently. As a result, an external authority – in this case literally the authorities – must correct the behavior of individual producers.

This is one of the clearest cases in which government intervention is desirable, even for economists. From the shared student kitchen to tuna fishing to traffic jam misery to CO_2 emissions: individual companies, producers, consumers or even entire countries do not succeed in internalizing the consequences of their actions for others.

THE SOLUTION: MORE MARKETS

The problem of global warming is perfectly described by this tragedy. Individual producers and even entire countries do not take the consequences of their actions for the worldwide environment sufficiently into account. The way in which the Chinese economy has evolved from that of a semi-developed country to one of the biggest environmental polluters in less than 25 years was only possible because no one was the owner of the atmosphere and so no one complained about there being too much pollution.

In practice there are various ways to tackle the 'tragedy of the commons'. They all amount to the same thing: each individual producer must in some way or another be made aware of the costs incurred for others. One solution is that the government determines exactly how much production can take place and thus exactly how much pollution or damage can be generated as a result. Although this seems like an attractive solution at first glance, in reality it is not. In the first place, it is as good as impossible for the government to determine the socially optimal quantity. It is not true that the government has superior information at its disposal and is capable of accurately deciphering all the riddles of nature or the planet. It is moreover unlikely that this optimal quantity is fixed and permanent: the unexpectedly rapid growth or shrinkage of the fish population, climatological circumstances, new fishing techniques or changing consumer preferences make the determination of *the* right quantity nearly impossible. Finally, maintaining government control over the exact amount of fish caught is also an immense task and will certainly generate costs of its own.

A second solution is the imposition of taxes. In the case of the tuna fishermen, a tax at the level of the vertical arrow would make the cost curve coincide exactly with the social cost curve. The price would increase and the total amount of fish caught would be reduced to the social optimum. The problem is still the same as above: it is not easy to determine exactly how much tax is needed to reach the social optimum. The most important objection, however, is that everyone is taxed in the same way. This is particularly problematic in the case of environmental pollution. In theory, both the most heavily polluting chemical company and the company with the most advanced environmental technology will have to pay the same tax per unit produced. The result is that both will have to reduce production, while we would actually prefer to have the heaviest polluter of the two produce less in exchange for the lesser polluter producing more.

The third solution takes on externalities at the root of the problem: the absence of property rights. Make everyone responsible for a piece of the common property and then everyone will alter his or her behavior. If we organize property rights correctly, we can clean up the mess. We can do this by privatizing the common property, for example. Instead of letting everyone graze the commons for free, we could sell the field to the highest bidder. Whoever wins and takes possession of the field can decide what to do with it: whose cattle may graze there, how much should be paid per cow and so on. The owner has every reason to maximize the profits from renting out the field, but at the same time, does not want to run the risk of overgrazing. He will therefore have to take into account costs as well as benefits. This was impossible when the field was common property. The interests of 'society' have become the interests of the individual. Although this solution seems attractive, it is difficult to carry out for a great many externalities. The ozone layer, the ocean, the entire fish population or the climate can hardly be privatized in practice.

A more practical solution is the allotment or auctioning of partial property rights. This amounts to dividing up and privatizing common property. In this way, fishing grounds can be allotted to individual fishermen, or common pastures assigned, sold or rented piece by piece to different farmers. This solution can also take the form of a fishing permit, pollution rights or CO_2 rights. In this way, you 'buy' pieces of fishing ground, the environment or the atmosphere, which can subsequently be resold or traded.

The emission of greenhouse gases would in theory lend itself perfectly to this solution. A company that takes it upon itself to produce more efficiently and in a way that is environmentally responsible will need less pollution rights. It can make even more money by selling its excess rights to another, less efficient company. Because the latter has much greater emissions for the same level of production, it needs more emission rights.

Trading in property rights is much more efficient than simply imposing a tax on everyone. It discourages pollution and encourages innovation and striving for efficient, sustainable solutions without the government intervening in the selection of the best technology. What is ingenious about this system of property or pollution rights is that the heaviest polluters are made responsible in every possible way. Either they invest in better production techniques, so that they save the money that would be spent on purchasing emission rights, or they significantly reduce production because the emission rights are too expensive. Or they shut down their facilities entirely and sell the remaining emission rights.

The most striking example of this kind of trade in pollution rights is the current European system of tradable CO_2 rights. This system, however, has turned into a complete fiasco. So many rights were allotted that the price collapsed, so that little or no trade in property or emission rights took place. The behavior of producers changed very little and the externalities continue to exist. That it is moreover a European system in answer to a planetary problem does not help matters either.

Nearly all economists, even the most rabid libertarians, recognize that externalities are the perfect textbook example of when government intervention is desirable. Essentially, environmental pollution, overfishing, and the risky management of a financial institution are not fundamentally different than neighbors fighting over a tree that creates too much shade. Common regulation of compensation or equal division of benefits and burdens is the only thing that can provide a solution in such situations. For this category of problems, there is certainly a role set aside for the government (see also the box "The role of the government" in chapter 6).

What does give rise to discussion is whether or not every externality justifies government intervention simply by definition. There are almost no human activities that do not have consequences for parties that are not involved. It is therefore possible to see externalities everywhere, and as a result, find reasons for government intervention everywhere. This is certainly not the idea. No one gets it into his head to have the government clean up the dirty student kitchen using taxes or regulations. It is something the students had best deal with among themselves by making clear and sensible agreements. The nightclub in a residential area can better make arrangements with the neighbors concerning opening hours, noise levels or financial compensation. As long as the problems are not on a planetary scale, it is more efficient when the perpetrators and the victims of harm discuss and resolve problems themselves. In this way, the market can still help overcome its own shortcomings.

Environmental pollution, overfishing, financial system risks and global warming are in no way consequences of the free market. The opposite is true: they are consequences of the absence of a market. Overfishing, environmental pollution and CO_2 emissions take place today without any immediately obvious consequences precisely because the fish population, the environment, the ozone layer and the climate belong to both no one and everyone. No one is the owner, no one feels responsible, and hence everyone can enjoy the advantages free of charge. In an apparent paradox, this free-market failure can best be remedied by the creation of a new market. The best outcome for society as a whole is to confront everyone with the actual social price of environmental pollution, financial system risks, energy consumption, overfishing and the like. Then everyone can react to the price stimuli for themselves.

SUBSIDIZE GOOD BEHAVIOR OR TAX BAD BEHAVIOR?

The proposal put forward by some politicians as the solution to the 'tragedy of the commons' is also not the best choice. Instead of artificially lowering the price of 'goods' with subsidies, it is better to calculate the real social price of the 'bads'. In this way, everyone is confronted with the actual social cost of energy consumption, environmental pollution or ecological footprints. Then everyone may choose individually how to deal with the higher prices. A rush-hour tax is more efficient for cutting down on traffic and pollution than subsidies for carpooling or taking the train. A higher price for electricity is more efficient for reducing energy consumption than subsidies for solar panels or wind turbines.

Subsidizing solar panels, wind turbines, electric cars and other 'better' technologies is only an illusory solution, one that is moreover very expensive. The subsidies take away the opportunity for the individual citizen or individual company to choose for themselves how they will have to deal with limited means. An environmental tax on 'dirty' sources of energy, for example, would be more efficient than subsidies for so-called 'clean' energy. A more expensive energy price would allow everyone to make their own choice: use energy more sparingly by setting the thermostat lower, moving to a smaller house, living in an apartment instead of a free-standing house, insulating walls, installing solar panels or a solar heater, using a heat pump, building a geothermal facility or ... with great pleasure, paying for the privilege of not changing anything at all. It is up to the individual citizen, consumer or producer to react to price signals. By making an arbitrary choice of one technology at the expense of another, subsidies distort the behavior of businesses and consumers. Their behavior will no longer be driven by what businesses and consumers actually want, but by the solution the government wants.

Moreover, subsidies act as a magnet for special interest groups that all find a reason why their product, service, activity or sector should receive subsidies. In other words: why their activity and their sector has a right to an unfair competitive advantage and the rest do not. 'The polluter pays' is very different compared to 'those who pollute less receive a subsidy'.

Nevertheless, there is still sufficient reason to be optimistic about the problem of externalities in general and environmental pollution in particular. The conviction is growing that polluters must pay for the pollution they create or the damage they cause. For planetary problems such as global warming, it will certainly be a challenge to come to an agreement, but there too improvement is on the horizon (see chapter 7).

The conclusion is clear: overfishing, environmental problems and global warming are not the consequences of too much market activity. On the contrary: they are symptomatic of the distressing absence of well-regulated property rights and a market for trading in them. The government must ensure that everyone is made responsible for externalities by means of the necessary price stimuli. Then it is up to the free market to react to those changing prices. So don't say "Who's going to clean up the kitchen today?" but: "Let's solve the tragedy of the commons through better allocation of property rights."

CLEARANCES ON THE HIGHWAY

Clearances: you can love them or hate them. Long lines, busy shopping malls, a stampede at clothing stores. When prices drop, demand rises. The number of stores remains the same in this case, but the number of purchasers suddenly skyrockets. That is the effect of prices that suddenly become structurally lower than the 'real' price.

Anyone who wants to have that special 'markdown feeling' on a regular day should try getting to Brussels from anywhere else in Belgium between six and nine in the morning. The number of kilometers of highway is still the same, but the number of highway users makes normal driving impossible. Whoever contemplates the situation while sitting in a traffic jam can only come to one conclusion: "The demand for public roads is currently higher than the supply." Anyone familiar with supply and demand knows that there can only be one explanation: the price paid is lower than the equilibrium price. Today, drivers only pay for private costs: registration tax, fuel, insurance and wear and tear on the car. At rush hour, however, the actual cost is much higher than the private cost. The actual cost encompasses lost work hours for everyone on the road, or environmental damage caused by inefficient fuel usage. Nobody pays for these extra costs at present.

This is the 'markdown feeling' in traffic: everyone is confronted with an apparently low price, such that there is much more demand for public roads than there is supply during peak hours. With traffic jams as a result.

Dozens of expensive campaigns have been launched over the years in an effort to fight traffic. Carpooling. Separate bus lanes. Free public transportation. Campaigns to encourage telework. In practice, none of these measures have met with much success. This should come as no surprise: to move consumers, punishment is more effective than reward. If someone has to pay the *actual* cost of moving from one place to another instead of just the private cost, it will have a much faster impact on the behavior of drivers. Rewards are particularly sympathetic, politically speaking, but they do little to help matters. Today, automobile traffic, freight traffic and public transportation are offered for less than the actual cost, in effect receiving subsidies. These subsidies impede consumer choice.

Traffic can only be dealt with effectively when the actual cost of rush-hour movement is passed on to the consumer. Raising fuel taxes is not really efficient. Then everyone would have to pay extra: those who swell traffic jams in the morning as well as those who drive at midnight along deserted highways. Intelligent tolls are probably a much better idea. They introduce a market where there wasn't one before: the available supply of highway is at any given moment confronted with the demand for highway. If there is an impending shortage, the equilibrium price increases. If plenty of highway space is available, the price can decrease – even drop to zero. Those who want to drive during rush hour may do so, but they will have to pay the price. The introduction of such a price will change the behavior of highway users.

The introduction of a price for moving from one place to another at different times of day or different times of the year, according to traffic flow or the amount of available space, could reconcile supply and demand perfectly.

The government could determine the price in terms of traffic flow, moment of the day or type of road. But it would be better to auction transportation rights or traffic rights among candidate drivers. Anyone who wants to drive on the Brussels ring road on a Monday morning between seven and nine will first have to purchase an electronic tag on a sort of eBay for transportation rights. The available supply of tags is always the same and is limited by the maximum capacity of the highway. Whether between seven and eight in the morning or eleven p.m. and midnight, there will always be the same amount of transportation rights on offer. The number of demanders, however, will differ significantly. Traveling on the ring roads of Brussels or Antwerp around midnight will be as good as free. Those who want to drive the same trajectory during the morning rush hour will have to pay a hefty price. This price gives the signal that there is scarcity and that it is necessary to use available space sparingly. Teleworking would suddenly become more interesting financially, as would carpooling or using public transportation. Employers would also be better able to attract employees if they could arrive at work for a minimum of expense. This is also the idea behind road pricing or the pay-as-you-drive system: getting users to pay for the obstruction they cause by providing price stimuli.

One argument put forward by opponents is that the use of tolls is unfair, particularly for individual transportation. Only affluent people would be able to afford a toll of three to seven euros for their daily commute. Driving without traffic as a luxury product seems to be beyond the pale for some people. As if collectively driving bumper-to-bumper without the distinction of rank or class somehow serves a higher egalitarian ideal. People stuck in traffic everywhere, unite! Social considerations should not play a role in indirect taxation. They are better served by a progressive income tax or redistribution policy. Unless we want bakers, barbers and bookstores to start charging an income-dependent value added tax.

A second criticism is that fuel today is already taxed enough. This income should already be sufficient for compensating the external costs involved. Alas! De Borger and Proost (2006) estimate that the actual cost of driving during rush hour is as much as two times higher than the privately paid cost. Today's fuel excise taxes are, moreover, not intelligent enough to combat traffic jams. Someone who uses the highway in the middle of the night does not cause traffic jams, but pays just as much fuel tax as someone who drives the same trajectory during the morning rush hour.

Finally: what if more and more people in the future drive electric cars? For a comparable trajectory they pay much less in taxes than those who are dependent on hydrocarbons. The subsidies they receive for purchasing their car even encourage them to drive more.

At the same time, in Belgium, almost nothing is taxed as heavily as labor. Things that are socially undesirable should be taxed. Things that are socially desirable can be subsidized. By allowing traffic to cause expensive traffic jams and environmental pollution 'for free', the government effectively subsidizes that traffic. A traffic jam subsidy, of all things! Where is the logic behind heavy taxes on labor and subsidies for traffic jams? Abolish the traffic jam subsidies and use the profits to make labor cheaper, among other things.

Now look around you again. On your dashboard you see the GPS transponder that keeps track of the cost of your current trajectory like a kind of personal taximeter. The device takes into account the time of day and location, and in this way, calculates the toll for your trip. You drive easily through traffic to your important meeting at a time that used to be known as 'rush hour'. From the cost displayed on the meter, you understand right away why other cars contain not only drivers, but also passengers who want to share the costs. You think that for that amount, you might as well take the train tomorrow. And the day after tomorrow you will work from a branch office in your neighborhood. Finally, you consider yourself lucky when you look around and see the good condition of the roads, which are well maintained in comparison to those in other countries. All because road pricing is still taboo there.

CHAPTER 5

More growth, better future

"Growth for the sake of growth is the ideology of the cancer cell." — **Edward Abbey**, American author (1927-1989) who was concerned with the environment.

"Without continual growth and progress, such words as improvement, achievement, success have no meaning." — **Benjamin Franklin**, American politician, scientist, and moralist (1706-1790)

"Continual fear and danger of violent death, and the life of man, solitary, poor, nasty, brutish and short." — **Thomas Hobbes**, English philosopher (1588-1679)

"Solitary, poor, nasty, brutish and short." So English philosopher Thomas Hobbes described the 'natural' condition of man in the pre-industrial age in the middle of the 17th century. As Adam Smith would later, Hobbes described the way human beings continually seek to better their lives. In contrast to Smith, however, Hobbes looked at the cup as half-empty rather than half-full, in a manner of speaking. According to him, humankind lives in a completely hostile environment in which everyone is out for profit at the cost of others. Each chance passer-by is a potential enemy. In such an environment, the most sensible option is thus to handle every fellow human being with a healthy degree of suspicion. With the result that his mistrust and enmity are thereby justified. And so on … and so on…

How do we reconcile this vision with the first chapter? There we assumed that enlightened self-interest leads to the improvement of everyone's welfare, and not to a constant battle of life and death. Even among the Aboriginals who lived thousands of years ago, we found evidence of 'trading man', who pursued his own self-interest and, in this way, enlarged the share of wealth for everyone. At the same time, human history as a whole is literally and figuratively packed with examples of 'mistrustful man'. Everywhere we go, we encounter boundless mistrust for one another: from battlefields to fortifications, from spears to bombers, from national borders to concentration camps and from instruments of torture to history books filled with unspeakable human suffering. Our history is a long succession of absolute highs and absolute lows. Highs in which a combination of confidence, innovation, freedom and free trade ensured growth and affluence, self-reinforcing confidence, wealth, progress and culture. But also absolute lows in which mistrust takes the upper hand and we torment one another in every possible way, cracking one another's skulls for the sake of food, territory, respect or power. During the better part of human history, long periods of mistrust, violence, repression and war dominated, only to be interrupted from time to time by periods of enlightenment and progress. Only to fall back into the old negative patterns once again.

Until around 200 years ago, the life of our ancestors looked exactly like this. Disease, war, repression, random violence, slavery, disfigurement, epidemics, hunger and poverty were the order of the day. To be born meant to expect a life as miserable as the life one's parents, grandparents and all the generations before had led. Political governance was characterized by arbitrariness, serfdom and slavery. These formed an extra millstone around the neck of the economy and supported an environment of near-zero growth. No one was interested in investing when a fellow citizen, aristocrat or prince could arbitrarily tax or even confiscate property. Those who either had no property or were not allowed to own it had no chance at all to make progress. Those who have no property rights – often not even the right to determine their own lives – cannot participate in a free market.

In short: there was nothing at all idyllic, romantic or idealistic about pre-industrial society. There was no growth and there was precious little to be happy about. The combination of a sky-high birth rate and a sky-high mortality rate kept the population in equilibrium. For every two children born, one failed to reach its fifth birthday. Society was, moreover, especially brutal: the annual number of murders in the middle ages is estimated at approximately 35 per 100,000 inhabitants, as apposed to 1.6 in present-day Belgium. In other words: across a period of two weeks in the middle ages, as many people were murdered as are now murdered in an entire year. Our forefathers lived a hard, poor, short life with no hope of improvement for the generations to come.

THE INVENTION OF GROWTH

For the better part of our history, our lifestyle has been one of 'stagnation'. The stagnation of life expectancy, of the economic environment and of the miserable standard of living. With no hope of improvement. Of course there were exceptions. Sometimes countries or regions progressed rapidly during a particular period of time. But this situation was inevitably followed by periods of decline, war, tyranny or disease. Illustration 8 shows perfectly how wealth per world inhabitant has developed over the last two millennia. After centuries of absolute economic standstill, wealth suddenly increased spectacularly at the end of the 18th century. In comparison to the centuries that went before, the acceleration of growth from the end of the 18th century onwards looks like nothing less than a rocket launch: it was the start of the first industrial revolution, which took place between 1760 and 1840. The invention of the steam engine, mechanized loom, steamship and steam locomotive, among other things, caused economic growth and the increase of wealth to go ... full steam ahead.

The sudden acceleration of economic growth ensured spectacular improvement in the standard of living. Innovations in the textile industry, metal industry and agriculture ensured cheaper clothing, while cheaper and easier agricultural products drastically reduced the chance of famine. Steam locomotives made transportation easier and cheaper, and opened up regions that had previously been left behind. The improvement in the standard of living worked as a fly-

Illustration 8: **Lift Off!**
Sources: Bradford DeLong, World Bank, author's own calculations

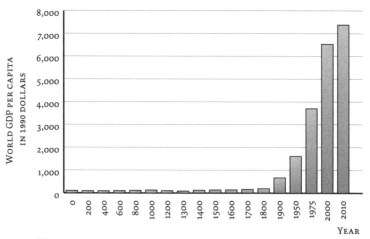

wheel for further economic growth: those who grew richer and lived longer could purchase more, produce more and were prepared to invest, thereby perpetuating economic growth.

Although the industrial revolution was in the first place a British phenomenon, progress also spread to the United States and the European mainland. Illustration 9 shows the evolution of wealth in Belgium over the past two millennia. From the beginning of human history it has taken at least 17 centuries for the standard of living of an inhabitant in this region to double. In the 19th century, by contrast, the standard of living doubled in less than a hundred years. Between 1900 and 2013, the average inhabitant of this country grew at least six times wealthier.

With the 'invention' of growth, two centuries of poverty came to an end. Why did this sudden leap in growth take so long? Why did the first industrial revolution take place in the 18th century and not in the 16th, or in the middle ages? A number of technological, social and political ingredients were needed, and all happened to come

Illustration 9: **Wealth in Belgium**
Source: Maddison (2007)

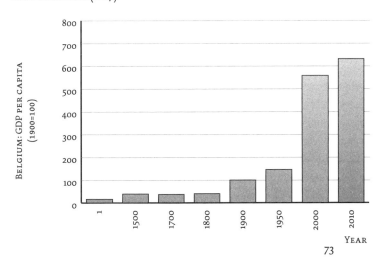

together at the right place. These ensured such a powerful economic cocktail that we progressed light years in a space of only two centuries'. A magic economic elixir for humanity.

Summed up briefly, these were the main ingredients:

Patent rights and property rights: one of the pacemakers of the first industrial revolution was the development of patent rights. Whoever made a discovery could from then on enjoy the profits of that discovery. It is not as if humankind only began to discover and innovate in the 18th century. Technological innovations had already taken place in the centuries before, but were never in fact the property of the inventor or developer. The protection of patents gave rise to an enormous competition of ideas and innovations that benefited society as a whole. The inventor was compensated for his invention, protected against imitation and society progressed as a result. New inventors for their part were stimulated to come forward with improvements to existing designs and, in this way, obtain their own patents. Pursuing enlightened self-interest in this way ensured constant competition between inventors, such that everyone improved: the inventors themselves and society as a whole. An environment in which property, investments, inventions or innovations can be confiscated at random is lethal to progress. This might sound obvious, but it is nevertheless one of the most important factors that slows down growth – in developing countries, for example.

Free market: an additional factor that ensured innovation and technological progress was the free market. What does it matter if one invents a mechanized loom if – as in the middle ages – the prince decides who may weave cloth, bake bread or forge iron? In the 18th and 19th centuries, Great Britain gradually reduced its protectionism and placed restrictions on monopolies and guilds. The liberation of the market gave everyone the right to compete and, in this way, became an extra pacemaker for innovation.

Limited liability and a culture of entrepreneurship: the possibility of setting up a company in which, in case of bankruptcy, you do not risk losing everything, encouraged risk-taking. A culture of entrepreneurship is also important: companies and consumers alike must be prepared to deal with change. It is not as if entrepreneurs and inventors decided they had had enough after the steam engine and the mechanized loom had been invented. On the contrary: the tempo of innovation and invention between 1750 and 1950 is nothing less than spectacular (see illustration 10).

Education, democracy and a stable political climate: growth only thrives in a stable physical and non-physical substrate. Roads, canals, ports, railroads and telecommunications networks are the physical infrastructure within which growth is possible. Education, democracy and a stable political climate are the non-physical infrastructure that makes growth possible. Greater access to education ensures a better educated population and in turn makes additional growth possible. Literacy combined with widely circulating newspapers ensured a more critical population, more political rights and gradual democratization in the West. An increasing number of democratic reforms ensured that the population could pluck the fruits of progress generated by the industrial revolution.

Between the pessimistic worldview of Hobbes and the world of today, our standard of living on the whole has increased spectacularly (see also illustration 9). Not even two world wars could stop the march of progress. From the experiences of the last two centuries we can also learn two major lessons: first and foremost, poverty is our natural condition. Second, the wealth we have been in the constant process of creating is built on self-interest (patent protection and the free market), risk (limited liability), freedom (democracy, the free market) and investment (education).

It was – in case there is any doubt – first and foremost the growth of the economy that made significant improvements to our standard of living possible. The higher standard of living in turn ensured lower child mortality and longer life expectancy in the long run. People who lived longer and grew richer demanded more freedom and political rights in order – in contrast to centuries previous – to be able to take part in the democratic process. People were no longer serfs or slaves, but participated in the market: as employees in the labor market, as consumers in the market for goods and services, as tenants or landlords in the housing market. Like it or not: citizens first acquired rights and riches as participants in the market. Rights and riches that they could subsequently transmute into demands for more political rights. The granting of freedoms or political rights did not occur because princes or political leaders suddenly came to great philanthropic insights of their own accord. It was primarily the merchants who felt prevented by the ruling elites from engaging in trade and therefore requested more rights.

It is important to remember that technological development, the free market, economic growth and the improvement of living standards always go hand in hand and have always reinforced one another. Technological development without the free market never gets out of the laboratory. Economic growth without the improvement of living standards is democratically untenable. And improving the standard of living is impossible without economic growth or technological development. All these elements are mutually dependent and self-reinforcing.

THE GROWTH OF WHAT?

What are we actually measuring when we talk about the growth of wealth? Often, we are most interested in the progress of society as a whole. Therefore we usually look at the gross domestic product per capita of the population. The gross domestic product is the total value of all goods and services that were delivered by an economy in one year. We then divide this amount by the total number of inhabitants of the country in question. This is the gross domestic product per capita of the population. We look at this figure as a measure of the average wealth of the population.

Let's take a simple example with two countries: Whiteland and Redland. Both are specialized in one activity: digging ditches. Whiteland and Redland each have 100 inhabitants. In both countries, each inhabitant has one shovel and is able to dig ten ditches a year. The gross domestic product – the gross domestic ditch, as it were – of both Whiteland and Redland is equal to 1,000. The wealth of both countries – the gross domestic product per inhabitant – is equal to 10.

The next year, the population of Redland increases by 20 people. They too have one shovel each and contribute to the total production. At the end of the year, the economy of Redland has grown to 1,200 ditches. The production of Whiteland is still the same as a year earlier: 1,000 ditches. Although the economy of Redland is now greater than that of Whiteland, the wealth per inhabitant has remained the same: 10 ditches per inhabitant.

Now let's see what happens in the third year: the population of Whiteland has replaced its 100 shovels with 100 digging machines. With a digging machine, each inhabitant can dig at least 40 ditches per year. Although there are still only 100 inhabitants, they have been able to dig a total of 4,000 ditches. In Redland nothing has changed: 120 inhabitants have dug a total of 1,200 ditches with their shovels. The gross domestic product of Whiteland is now noticeably higher than that of Redland. Its total wealth has increased four times over.

The gross domestic product per inhabitant has also grown four times over, from 10 ditches to 40.

Finally, let's see what happens in year four. Redland continues to swear by its traditional shovels and its population does not grow. The result is that production levels – the gross domestic product – remain the same at 1,200 ditches per year. In Whiteland people are convinced that, thanks to the introduction of digging machines, not everyone has to work. It is decided that only 60 inhabitants have to work, while the remaining 40 can spend more time enjoying life. As a result, after one year only 2,400 ditches are dug. This is less than the year before, but still more than in Redland. The per capita income of the population in Whiteland is equal to 24 – more than double Redland's 10. In other words: in spite of the fact that nearly twice as many people are employed in Redland, both their total production and the per capita wealth of the population is smaller than in Whiteland.

The growth of productivity or innovation ensures that the same number of people can do more work. Or to put it a different way: the same level of production can be realized with fewer people (see also chapter 8). In general, then, there are two ways in which the total wealth of a country can grow: population growth and productivity growth. In order to ensure the growth of per capita wealth, productivity growth and innovation are determining factors. They are the core reactor of progress; they create wealth.

In the meantime it is clear that innovation leads to improvements in productivity. It is precisely these improvements in productivity that are the engine of increased wealth. The three examples below demonstrate this quite clearly:

» Before the arrival of running water and sewage systems, women were responsible for providing fresh water and removing waste-water from the household. Historical documents from the United States give us a good idea of just how big a job this was. In 1885, the average housewife in North Carolina carried an average of 35 tons of water over a distance of more than 200 kilometers every year. For health, life expectancy and the emancipation of women, it is difficult to imagine a more important milestone than the introduction of running water and sewage systems.

» Before the advent of the steam engine or the internal combustion engine, horses were the most important suppliers of power on a large scale. The transportation of people and shipments between and within cities always relied on horses. The unsavory result: per square kilometer, each city had to process two to four tons of manure a day, which had to be removed, of course. Manually.

» Finally, the impact of an invention like the internal combustion engine on standards of living and productivity can hardly be overestimated. To reach the equivalent of the amount of energy contained in a single barrel of oil, an average man would have to engage in physical labor every day for eight years. In other words: the physical effort of an exhausting 40 years of work as a wood-cutter is consolidated in a scant five barrels of oil. That is the essence of economic growth, wealth and human progress.

Illustration 10: **Industrial revolution...**
Source: Gordon (2012)

When?	What?	Made possible...
1750-1830	steam engine mechanized loom steam locomotive steamship	railroads, canals, mechanized agriculture, lower food prices, urbanization, widely circulated newspapers, democratization, labor unions...
1870-1900	electricity electric lighting internal combustion engine running water sewage systems	all electric applications for consumers: elevators, radios, telephones, household appliances, refrigerators, cars, trucks, airplanes, road networks, opening up of rural areas, commuting, supermarkets, highways, synthetics, telecommunications, air-conditioning...
1960-...	computer mainframe Internet	automated telephone traffic, electronic payment systems, text editing, space travel, democratization of air travel, scientific progress thanks to computing power, supply management, paperless offices, online stores...

In general, history is full of examples of improvements to productivity and innovation that ensure greater wealth. Each of the examples in the brief list below has caused an increase in wealth. Illustration 10 systematically depicts just how the industrial revolution led to a wealth revolution. In chapter 8 we will examine further the broader implications of higher productivity on wealth and employment.

- » exchanging a shovel for a digging machine;
- » replacing a dirt road with a paved road;
- » mechanizing a production line;
- » making a population literate;
- » inoculating children against polio;
- » replacing letters with email;
- » replacing a post-chase with a telegram;
- » replacing telegrams with telephones;
- » replacing an abacus with a calculator;
- » replacing an ox with a tractor;
- » replacing natural fertilizer with artificial;
- » replacing water pumps with water pipes;
- » ...

WHY DO WE NEED GROWTH?

Over the past 200 years, the standard of living – particularly in the West – has risen spectacularly. Some people ask themselves today whether we still need growth per se. They equate 'growth' or 'economic growth' with materialism, the erosion of norms and values, consumerism, growing inequality, the plundering of nature, global warming, environmental pollution, shopping addictions, large shopping malls, obesity and all the rest of the diseases associated with wealth. This is a major misconception. Admittedly, without growth we would never have had large shopping malls. Nor would we have traffic jams, obesity, materialism, Hollywood blockbusters, supermarkets, shopping centers, excessive commercials on TV and certainly no Internet. At the same time, however, we would never have had healthcare, freedom, social security, road networks, public education, environmental regulation, culture, annual vacation ... the list goes on and on.

That we all have to work much fewer hours today than a hundred years ago is thanks to growth. That child mortality has never been lower is thanks to growth. That we have been able to develop a social security system is thanks to growth. That some countries have been able to expand their education systems is thanks to growth. That we can use tax money for the redistribution of wealth is thanks to growth. Growth for growth's sake is not the goal; growth makes other things possible. Growth is a means that gives people, companies or countries the ability to improve their lot. What they do with that growth and how they arrange their priorities is entirely up to them.

An increase in total wealth in countries like Saudi Arabia or Qatar might be used to build ski slopes in the desert, luxurious shopping malls or a paved Formula 1 circuit. China might use greater wealth to invest in foreign building terrain, buy French vineyards, set up a social security system or build an aircraft carrier. A country like Sweden will probably use an increase in wealth for more social safety nets, a shorter workweek or better environmental protection. In the United States, an increase in wealth might be deployed in expanding the Department of Defense or Homeland Security or perhaps reducing taxes. Growth is not an end in itself: what counts is what that growth enables a society to do.

The same goes for individuals. When people make financial progress, they will all make their own individual choices. Some will use the money to purchase more consumer goods or a bigger car or to eat in restaurants more often or go on vacation. Others will save in order to give the money to their children or grandchildren. Still others will purchase expensive bio products, pay membership dues to Greenpeace or give direct financial support to the third world.

We can lament some of these choices. Or perhaps we have our own, better ideas about how greater wealth should be spent. But in order to make those choices, we first need growth. Whether it is about better education, more healthcare, a lower retirement age, more defense spending, less environmental pollution, more work, culture subsidies or lower taxes ... without growth, a society cannot better itself.

When it comes to poor countries, nearly everyone agrees that growth is necessary. There, economic growth and increased prosperity are sometimes a question of life and death. Illustration 11 shows the enormous differences in wealth in the present-day global economy. An average American has an average income of nearly 50,000 dollars. At the other extreme we find a country like Congo, with an average annual income of just over 300 dollars. Put another way: one American is richer than an entire medium-sized Congolese village.

Probably the best answer as to why poor countries need economic growth in the first place is the Preston curve (see illustration 12). It depicts the link between income per capita of the population and life expectancy. As intuition might suggest, a higher per capita income leads to an increase in life expectancy. However, it is among the poorest countries that the effect of growth is strongest. Even a very small increase in per capita income adds up to an immense improvement in the quality of life. From the moment that wealth in a country dramatically increases, its effect on life expectancy is less pronounced.

Illustration 11: **From dirt poor to filthy rich**
Source: International Monetary Fund,
World Economic Outlook Database (April 2013)

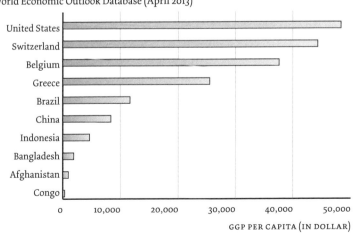

GGP PER CAPITA (IN DOLLAR)

Although an average Japanese citizen is wealthier than an average Spaniard, their life expectancy is more or less the same. Particularly in the poorest countries, growth is literally and figuratively of vital importance. It illustrates once more that growth for growth's sake is senseless: growth is there to improve people's quality of life.

For the poorest countries today, achieving economic growth is in the first place a matter of health, child mortality, and life expectancy. But for them it doesn't end there. The will and the desire to improve one's own lot do not end with higher life expectancy. Just look at China. First and foremost, market reforms there have resulted in uninterrupted record growth for the last two decades. That economic growth has lifted hundreds of millions of Chinese out of absolute poverty within one generation. That in itself undoubtedly makes it one of the most successful development programs in human history, and in terms of effectiveness greatly surpasses traditional forms of development aid. Look at the experience of the average Chinese. He is not only more affluent than his parents, but he also wants even

Illustration 12: **Preston-curve**
Source: Deaton, Angus (2003), Health, inequality, and economic development, *Journal of Economic Literature, Vol. XLI, pp. 113-158*

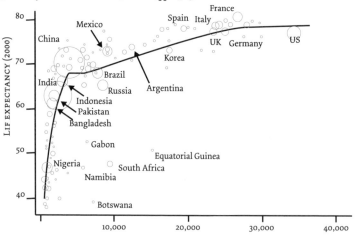

INCOME PER CAPITA (IN DOLLAR, 2000)

more progress. In great numbers, he drinks Starbucks, wears Nike, uses an iPhone and drives a BMW or Mercedes. And if he doesn't, he at least has the ambition to someday.

Shopping malls, McDonald's, a widescreen television, Coca-Cola or a large American refrigerator are dismissed or disdained by many wealthy Westerners, as if they were symbols of 'vulgar' consumerism. For millions of people in developing countries, however, they are a cherished dream and symbols of freedom, affluence and economic progress. There is also a reason why people from extremely poor and repressive countries flee to the 'rich West' in great numbers. They prove that Adam Smith's arguments still hold true: people pursue their enlightened self-interest. For one reason or another Westerners are willing to make allowances for this in the case of poor refugees. But when it comes to the Westerners themselves, it is not good form to claim that self-interest plays a role in their daily activities. Nevertheless it is so: people primarily want to improve their lot and that of their children. And because for many impoverished people, the society or economy in which they live does not offer them the freedom to pursue their enlightened self-interest, they seek this possibility in the wealthy West. Migration waves of economic refugees are therefore the best proof that the overwhelming majority of humanity is looking for growth and progress.

DO WEALTHY COUNTRIES NEED GROWTH?

For wealthy countries it is apparently much more difficult to defend the position that they still need economic growth. "We already have more than enough", or "the earth cannot afford our lifestyle", are frequently heard arguments that plead against economic growth. The wealthier the country, the more economic growth or an increase in affluence or progress is viewed as a luxury product. For some it is even perverse to think that the West still wants to pursue growth. Nevertheless, even wealthy countries need growth if their societies are to make progress. And it is not as if choosing in favor of progress is less valid for a wealthy country than a poor one.

Without growth, the pie of wealth to go around remains the same size – it's just that it becomes harder to give everyone a fair share. The progress of one is inevitably at the expense of another. Fighting poverty leads to cuts in public transportation; more social safety nets have to be financed by having less culture. A new bridge has to be paid for by higher taxes or lower pensions or less money for environmental protection. Without growth, our nose is rubbed in the fact that affluence is finite. A society that does not grow is one in which individual citizens, entrepreneurs and demographic groups are ranged against one another.

When a country's wealth grows, it is easier to share the wealth. The middle class and the wealthiest members of society will be more willing to share some of their wealth if they know that they themselves will still be better off. By contrast, a stagnating society is not only more closed, it will more than likely start rejecting the idea of redistributing wealth and become less democratic. Societies in which the economy is growing are more open, incline more toward democracy and equality and are more ambitious.

The ample presence of economic growth also explains why we have made so much progress on nearly all possible levels over the last few decades. Even in comparison to the recent past – the 1960s and 1970s – life is much better today. We have become wealthier and better educated; we live longer and are healthier, smoke less and are more environmentally conscious. Cars are safer, use less fuel and therefore pollute less. Industry is more aware of its ecological responsibility, meaning that our living environment is improving as a result. Nearly everyone's standard of living has increased. Telecommunication, transportation, vacation, leisure time ... are available for many more people. All that progress is only there thanks to growth. We have only succeeded in combining so many different projects (comfort, quality of life, health, social safety nets, environment, equality, individual wealth and affluence) because there was economic growth. If our financial welfare had stagnated in the meantime, we would not have been able to make such a great leap forward in any of those areas.

If you could choose, where would you most like to live? Which society offers a citizen the most chances to improve his or her lot? Where will people have the most chances of progressing in the years to come? Rapidly growing Turkey or declining Greece? Poor, stagnating North Korea or wealthy, growing South Korea? Poor but rapidly growing Angola or poor and stagnating Zimbabwe? The United States or the Eurozone?

Growth offers a society and all its members a chance at a better life. Growth creates chances. For everyone. What we use that growth for differs from country to country and from citizen to citizen. Naturally the political and social priorities of Belgium are drastically different from those of contemporary Afghanistan. Or even from those of Belgium in the 19th century. The suppression of infectious diseases such as small pox, measles, diphtheria and polio is no longer the order of the day. Women's literacy is a goal we have already achieved, as is universal access to education. Further increasing life expectancy is also less of a top priority than it used to be. Our preferences are now very different: fighting child poverty, research into Alzheimer's, development aid, unemployment among unskilled workers, a better functioning currency, fighting cancer, better integration of immigrants in society and the labor market, tolerance, fighting marginality, a broader dissemination of culture, a cleaner environment, research into rare diseases... Although the priorities of every country will differ, economic growth is always necessary in order to achieve them. That is the most important message.

Those who reject growth, reject progress. In an environment without growth, a step forward for one always means a step backward for another. A stagnating economy creates a society of 'either/or'. Growth makes 'and/and' possible. To sum up: a society without growth is a society without ambition. A society without ambition is a society without growth.

CHAPTER 6

Growth or equality?

"*Even the striving for equality by means of a directed economy can result only in an officially enforced inequality – an authoritarian determination of the status of each individual in the new hierarchical order.*"
— Friedrich Hayek

"*The smallest minority on earth is the individual. Those who deny individual rights cannot claim to be defenders of minorities.*" **— Ayn Rand**

"*A society that puts equality before freedom will get neither. A society that puts freedom before equality will get a high degree of both.*" **— Milton Friedman**,
American economist (1912-2006), advocate of the free market and Nobel Prize winner

What is more important: growth or equality? Is it more important that everyone makes progress, or is the progress of some more important than the progress of others? Is more wealth the best way to more equality? Or does more wealth simply create a more unequal distribution of that same wealth?

Whenever we refer to inequality in practice, people intuitively think of poverty. Those who try to imagine an unequal society, generally think of stinking rich jetsetters at the top of the distribution of income and dirt poor paupers at the bottom.

When we want to measure absolute poverty in a society, we should look at the number of people that have to get by with less than one dollar per day, the number of people who live on less than 2,000 calories per day, the number of people that have no access to education or medical care. In practice, the West is so prosperous that this form of absolute poverty – dying of hunger, deprivation, or disease – is a marginal phenomenon.

For this reason, in practice we do not measure *absolute* poverty in the West, but *relative* poverty. To measure poverty, the European statistics bureau Eurostat, for example, relies exclusively on relative criteria. Eurostat says in its 2010 annual *Yearbook on Poverty and Exclusion* that "the EU's concept of monetary poverty is based on relative measures." In the work of the Centrum voor Sociaal Beleid (Center for Social Policy) at the University of Antwerp – in effect the benchmark for poverty research in Belgium – this current European definition is also used. In concrete terms, the poverty line is defined as 60% of the most average income of the income ranking. Those who earn less than 60% of the most average income – the median income – are considered poor. Among other things, this means that the poverty line will be different in every country – precisely because it is not based on an absolute figure, but on the structure of the total distribution of income. Estimated poverty will therefore differ significantly from country to country. According to Eurostat's figures for 2011 you are poor in Bulgaria, for example – as a family with two young children – if you earn less than 7,180 EUR per year. In Belgium, you are poor if you earn less than 22,673 EUR, and in Luxembourg you have to earn less than 33,600 EUR to be considered poor. By constructing poverty standards in this way, inequality is almost automatically translated as poverty. When we speak of 'poverty' in the West, we are not usually talking about absolute deprivation, but lagging behind in comparison to a relative measure such as a median.

It is important to keep in mind the difference between *absolute* and *relative* poverty. After all, this way of measuring poverty has great consequences for economic policy. By measuring Western 'poverty', one is in practice measuring "inequality." There are two important reasons for this. In the first place, "poverty" is a much more loaded concept than 'inequality'. If you want to mobilize people, you would do much better to use the word 'poverty' than the word 'inequality'. In other words: an article about 'poverty in Belgium' will be much more likely to make the front page of a newspaper than an article about 'inequality in Belgium'. In the second place, absolute poverty – in the sense of absolute deprivation of food, housing or medical care – is as good as non-existent in the West. The social battle for the reduction of absolute poverty has already been fought here. As a result, the new theater of operations is the reduction of what we know as relative poverty. The concrete consequence is that when action groups or political parties engage themselves for the cause of reducing poverty, they are actually fighting for more equality.

FIVE-PERSON COUNTRY: WEALTHY BUT UNEQUAL

In order to show clearly how relative poverty, wealth, growth and inequality are related, we will analyze two simple societies: Five-Person Country and New Five-Person Country.

In Five-Person Country there are – how could it be otherwise – five citizens. They have a respective income of 300, 200, 100, 80 and 50. The country is on average quite wealthy, but its income distribution is unequal: the wealthiest citizen earns six times more than the poorest. The most average citizen earns 100 – the median income of Five-Person Country. The poverty line is set at 60% by taking the median income. In concrete terms, the poverty line is thus equal to 60. In concrete terms, there is one citizen in five who earns below the poverty line. One fifth of the population is therefore considered poor. Imagine now that next year, the economy of Five-Person Country grows considerably: its total wealth increases by 10%. Moreover, everyone is able to profit equally from this considerable progress: everyone earns 10% more than a year ago. The new income distribution is now 330, 220, 110, 88, and 55. The new median income is now 110. The poverty line is still set at 60% of the median income. Given that the median income has risen to 110, the poverty line has also risen to 66.

Again this means that one in five citizens has an income below the poverty line. Just like a year ago. This conclusion is striking: in spite of the fact that the material well-being of everybody in Five-Person Country has increased by 10%, the percentage of poverty remains unchanged. One in five citizens can still be considered poor. From the richest to the poorest, everyone's situation has improved, and everyone can afford a higher absolute standard of living. But according to relative poverty standards, poverty in Five-Person Country is still a problem. Those who are interested in absolute progress are happy with an income increase of 10%. Those who are primarily concerned with poverty or inequality find that nothing has changed.

This is the paradox of this widely used method of calculating poverty. It has nothing to do with effective deprivation, hunger or an effective lack of opportunities. It focuses on income distribution or income inequality. The most perverse consequence is that according to adepts of this approach, poverty will never be resolved by ensuring more economic growth, progress or wealth. That the poorest citizens have progressed 10% and can afford more than last year does not matter to adherents of this method. The results are poor because income distribution has not been compressed. On the contrary: the absolute difference between the wealthiest and the poorest inhabitant of Five-Person Country has even increased. The difference was 250, and after the 10% growth in income, the absolute difference between the wealthiest and poorest increased to 275. So the difference between wealthy and less wealthy in absolute terms increased by 10%. You can repeat this exercise with an income increase of 20, 200 or 2,000%. In spite of the spectacular increase in absolute wealth for everyone, poverty in Five-Person Country will always remain fixed at 20%. The median income rises with all the other incomes. The poorest 20% continue to chase the poverty line without being able to get past it.

This is also an essential characteristic of the agenda of most Western opponents of poverty: for them, growth is never a recipe for less poverty. Only redistribution of wealth can combat poverty in their opinion. Or: only a compression of income distribution is in their view a true blow against poverty. The very means by which poverty is measured also betrays quite clearly the way adherents of this view hope to fight poverty. This will become even clearer in the example of a neighboring country.

Illustration 13: **Rich versus unequal**

	Five-Person Country		New Five-Person country	
	year 1	year 2	year 1	year 2
citizen 1	300	330	50	45
citizen 2	200	220	50	45
citizen 3	100	110	50	45
citizen 4	80	88	50	45
citizen 5	50	55	50	45
Poverty line	60	66	30	27
Percentage of poor people	20%	20%	0%	0%
Total wealth	730	803	250	225
Wealth per capita	146	160.6	50	45

Let us imagine another country with five citizens: New Five-Person Country. A model country in which fighting poverty and the equality of citizens occupies pride of place. In New Five-Person Country there are again five citizens. This time they all have the same income. Everyone earns 50, not by chance the income of the poorest citizen in our first example. The average per capita income of the population, however, is noticeably lower than in Five-Person Country. There, the average income per inhabitant was 146, while in New Five-Person Country it is only around a third of that. The median income in New Five-Person Country is, of course, equal to 50, and thus the poverty line is located at 30 (60% of 50).

The conclusion is also clear: in New Five-Person Country there are no poor people! Everyone earns above the poverty line; therefore the percentage of poverty amounts to 0%. The total wealth of New Five-Person Country may be but a fraction of that of Five-Person Country, but apparently poverty does not exist. Note, too, that the citizen of Five-Person Country who earns the least is considered poor in that country. In New Five-Person Country, however, he is well above the poverty line and, as a result, would not be considered poor.

In order to drive the point home, we can even include a decrease in total wealth. Imagine that at a given moment, the total wealth of New Five-Person Country drops by 10%. Everyone shares in the misfortune and all incomes decrease from 50 to 45. Even without having to make calculations, it is clear that there are still no poor people. Everyone still earns the same as everyone else, and so everyone still earns above 60% of the median income. The total wealth of the community has collapsed, but there is still no poverty.

It should be clear: this way of defining poverty creates many problems. First and foremost, the measures used will ensure that an absolute increase in the standard of living – through more economic growth – will never be translated into a reduction in poverty. If the concept of 'poverty' is derived from 'inequality', poverty can only be lowered when the distribution of income is compressed. Secondly, this sort of measurement leads to absurd findings. Those who measure relative poverty will find that poverty in the wildly wealthy city-state of Monaco has hit record highs. Not because the average émigré soccer player, cyclist or Formula 1 racecar driver is in danger of dying from hunger or thirst, but because income distribution between rich, mega-rich and ultra-rich is distorted.

Is growth more important than poverty or is it the other way around? Should poverty be defined as an absolute level of deprivation or as a relative inequality of income? There is no conclusive answer, let alone a clear definition of precisely what poverty or inequality is. It is up to each individual to make this choice in all good conscience. What is clear is that the current manner of measuring poverty will push redistribution rather than growth as the solution. Nevertheless, growth remains the most effective way of fighting poverty effectively. This is evident in numerous studies. David Dollar and Aart Kraay of the World Bank have irrefutably shown in 2002 and again in 2013 that the evolution of the incomes of the poorest is most strongly correlated with the growth of the entire economy. The conclusion is also clear: a policy that seeks to fight poverty should put its money on economic growth and the creation of wealth.

GROWTH ENSURES EQUALITY AND INEQUALITY

For those who put their money on fighting inequality, by contrast, growth per se can never be the solution. And those who want to realize maximum growth had best shut their eyes to inequality. In practice, an increase in wealth will lead in the first phase to an increase in income inequality. In the second phase, additional growth will ensure that this same income inequality decreases (see illustration 14).

It was the Nobel Prize winner Simon Kuznets (1901-1985) who first observed this phenomenon. He found that in very poor societies, inequality was relatively low. Everyone was more or less badly off to the same extent, and income differences were in general relatively limited. When a society becomes wealthier, inequality increases. In a phase of rapid growth, not everyone progresses at the same rate. In this phase, talent, access to financial means or the ruling class primarily determines who will get ahead. If these factors are unevenly distributed at the beginning, the increase in wealth throughout society will also be unevenly distributed. Wealth as a whole increases at lightning speed, but not everyone profits from it to the same degree. This is a phenomenon we see today in countries such as Brazil, Mexico and China.

Beginning at a particular income level, attention to inequality increases and redistribution becomes more important. That moment is usually the moment at which the average citizen has also become the average voter. From then on, a citizen can always show that he or she finds redistribution important, which in turn ensures that it becomes a political priority. The wealthiest Western countries are now in the phase in which inequality ranks among the lowest in the world. Belgium, for example, is one of the countries in which inequality has decreased most in the last few decades. The heightened focus on redistribution, however, has increasingly come at the cost of focusing on wealth as a whole.

Redistribution and less inequality are in themselves laudable objectives. In the first place, they certainly make a society more harmonious and more stable. But always choosing more equality is not without consequences. The large degree of redistribution demanded by the voters or by society can only be instituted in practice through heavy taxes on the upper side of the income distribution curve and heavy subsidies on the lower side. This combination of taxes and subsidies lowers a society's potential for creating growth.

Just look at the example of Five-Person Country. In this society – with unequal income distribution that is relatively limited when all is said and done – the average income is 146. Now imagine that – in the name of equality – we want to ensure that ultimately, everyone has the same income. We could do that by levying taxes in order to finance income subsidies. To reduce the income of the wealthiest citizen from 300 to 146, we would have to tax his original income at more than 50%. To increase the income of the poorest citizen from 50 to 146, he would have to receive an income subsidy that is nearly double the amount of his income before the transfers. It is immediately clear that the hefty taxes – and associated transfers put a serious dent in the appetite for entrepreneurship, the creation of wealth and growth. The highest earning inhabitant of Five-Person Country retains less than half of his efforts, labor and entrepreneurship, and will probably be less inclined to work much harder. After all, of everything that he earns, more than half goes to the collective. The same holds true for the poorest inhabitant. Working or starting a new enterprise cannot possibly secure the same progress as what he receives through the transfers. The transfers also reduce his readiness to work more or harder. As we see from the above example,

Illustration 14: **Kuznets curve**

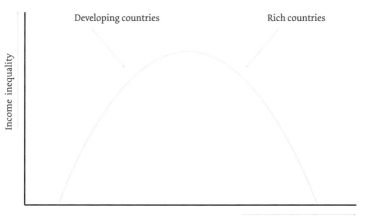

taxes and income subsidies both reduce readiness to work and have a negative effect on the creation of wealth. For both rich and poor. For those who pay taxes as well as for those who receive income subsidies.

This is the contemporary paradox for many Western countries. Too great an inclination towards equality destroys the underlying potential for the economy to grow. The more the focus is on redistribution of wealth, the less wealth there will be to distribute. Just pulling out a knife to cut the pie and announcing that pie will be served is enough to make the pie shrink. Those who continue to focus even more intently on redistribution in an environment of shrinking wealth bite the hand that feeds them. The most creative and most entrepreneurial citizens – the most heavily taxed citizens – will be further discouraged from contributing to the whole. The least creative and least talented citizens – the most heavily subsidized – will likewise be less inclined to contribute to the whole. The solution of this problem in the coming years will be equivalent to squaring the circle. Will we decide in favor of more growth and affluence, thereby tempering the inclination toward equality and redistribution? Or will the drive toward ever-increasing redistribution of wealth permanently undermine the creation of that very wealth?

AN ALTERNATIVE TO REDISTRIBUTION?

All of these findings are not in themselves an argument against redistribution. Too much inequality is, of course, undesirable. In a society in which inequality is too pronounced, the great difference between the haves and have nots makes normal life impossible. On the other hand, too much striving for equality on the basis of redistribution undermines the growth potential of the economy. It is a balancing act not to fall into one of the two extremes. Apart from that, there is the question as to whether financial redistribution alone can ever be a real answer to poverty. Those who want to fight poverty must trust in the capacities of each individual – rather than compensating them for a presumed lack of capacities by means of redistribution.

98

It therefore seems best to bet on a two-pronged policy. On the one hand there is a group of people whose mental and physical limitations will always make it difficult for them to survive without help. Redistribution is essential for offering protection to the weakest members of society. Financial and material support is necessary for people who cannot get by without help from others.

For everybody else on the lower end of society, education and training should be the most important weapons in the fight against poverty. Poverty is often caused by lack of education, training or schooling. Access to better or better-paying jobs is often determined on the basis of ability and productivity. Education and training are thus central pillars in every policy that deals with poverty (see box "The role of government"). Although income subsidies and redistribution can give people a head start in trying to get ahead, redistribution alone is insufficient for really fighting poverty. It not only destroys all initiatives that might induce people to take initiatives for themselves, it is an underestimation of everyone's capacities for getting ahead on their own. Only through more and better education will people really have the chance to improve their own situation and escape from poverty. More education ensures more wealth, and more wealth benefits everyone. More education for the poorest members of society ensures higher productivity, a better job and a higher salary, and as a result, is the only sustainable way to help them escape poverty.

The role that the government plays in a modern society has become greater and more important in the last few hundred years. Today, most Western countries – namely, Western Europe – have what is undoubtedly the largest average government, measured in terms of government expenditure as a percentage of total wealth. One can hardly think of an area of life in which the government doesn't play a role today.

Nevertheless, a country without government is hardly to be recommended. Countries with a dysfunctional government, or even without a government, do not perform well in general. In terms of life expectancy, wealth per inhabitant, violence or human rights, they are nearly always on the wrong end of international rankings. Look at a country like Somalia, for example, one of the few countries in the world today that does not have a central government. Living in such an environment is hardly a walk in the park. Without a central authority that establishes and enforces rules, society degenerates into complete anarchy: a continual struggle of everybody against everybody else in which the law of the strongest always prevails. In Somalia, a conflict over a goat that has been traded, a disputed piece of land, or a sealed marriage pact will not be handled by a judge, but by vengeance, attack, abuse or murder.

This was how our lives looked for a better part of human history. Fortunately we have evolved in the meantime and are no longer subject to the law of the strongest. Without enforceable laws, a deployable police force and independent judges, modern society could scarcely function. This is also the most essential role of government: establishing rules. Citizens may then – within the valid rules – make contracts with one another in all freedom. It is the government's job to enforce these contracts.

Another important role for the government is the provision of 'public goods'. These are goods that are not offered on the free market – or at least not in sufficient quantities. Not because they are not good for our welfare – on the contrary. Public goods are particularly useful, but once offered nobody may be barred from accessing them. Take a lighthouse, for example. Building a lighthouse and offering it on the free market by asking subscription money from all those who want to use it would be unthinkable. Once the lighthouse is built and in use, every ship may use its signals and in practice no ship can be excluded. Other examples include fortifications, road networks, dykes, fresh air and police protection. Trains, postal service, telephone operators, package delivery services, airlines and housing, by contrast, are not pure public goods. It is precisely because no one can claim ownership of public goods that they will not be offered on the free market, and as a result, it is up to the government to provide them. In order to be able to provide these goods, the government needs income, which it will collect in the form of taxes.

Externalities also justify government intervention. In chapter 4 we saw how negative externalities formed a textbook example of when government intervention becomes necessary. Negative externalities are harmful goods that, without government intervention, would be offered in large quantities – precisely because their suppliers do not take into account the negative consequences of their behavior on others. Typical examples include overfishing, environmental pollution, excessive noise, CO_2 emissions or traffic. It is up to the government to pass on the social costs to those who pollute or otherwise deal in negative goods, and in this way, limit the damage.

There is also such a thing as positive externalities, and these also require government intervention. While in the case of negative externalities there is too much of something damaging on offer, with positive externalities, just the opposite is true: there is too little of something useful on offer, because each individual takes insufficient account of the positive effects for others when making a decision. Take vaccination, for example. By having yourself vaccinated against an infectious disease, you lower not only your own chances of contracting the disease, but also those of the people around you, since you can no longer infect them. Because everyone would consider only his or her own chances of getting sick in a free market, fewer people would be vaccinated than socially optimal. Just as it is the government's task to discourage harmful behavior, it is also its job to encourage useful behavior. This means that it gives the individual citizen a nudge in the right direction. Other examples of positive externalities include education as well as research and development. The advantages of education and research and development benefit the entire society and not just the individual citizen or individual company.

It is also on this basis, for example, that a universal system of health insurance or redistribution of wealth can be defended. In a completely private system, some people would probably be underinsured against disease or misfortune, with dire consequences as a result. Others would be overinsured, with medical inflation as a result. In themselves these are also market imperfections – incomplete information, bad information – against which the government acts. An additional argument in favor of redistribution is that excessive inequality gives occasion to more crime or social unrest, and in this way, slows down the growth of total wealth. Redistribution is also a way of improving social stability, so that the creation of wealth is made easier.

In short, the role of the government can be summed up as follows: establishing and enforcing rules, providing public goods, collecting taxes to finance them, discouraging harmful social behavior and encouraging useful social behavior. It is against this touchstone that government policy must be tested.

CHAPTER 7

The earth will not implode

---

*"It is not that people started breeding like rabbits,
they just stopped dying like flies."*
— Anonymous UN official

*"Without a true world government to control reproduction
and the use of available resources, the sharing ethic of
the spaceship is impossible. For the foreseeable future,
our survival demands that we govern our actions by the
ethics of a lifeboat, harsh though they may be."*
— Garrett Hardin, American ecologist (1915-2003)

"Necessity is the mother of invention."
— Plato, Greek philosopher (427-347 BC)

*"Our problems are manmade; therefore, they can be solved
by man. And man can be as big as he wants. No problem of
human destiny is beyond human beings."*
— John F. Kennedy (1917-1963), former president of
the United States of America (1961-1963)

*"I think we're going to the moon because it's in the nature of
the human being to face challenges. It's by the nature of his
deep inner soul ... We're required to do these things just as
salmon swim upstream."* **— Neil Armstrong**,
the first man on the moon (1930-2012)

One million people. Double the size of Queens and about half of Brooklyn. This was the approximate population of the world before the invention of agriculture around 12,000 years ago. Before that it was even smaller. Human beings were simply one of many life forms on the earth. For the better part of human history, the population scarcely increased. Shrinking or expanding was determined by natural circumstances: disease, war, conflict, the quantity and quality of the food supply. Two decades before Belgium declared its independence, the world reached one billion inhabitants for the first time. It had taken nearly the whole of human history to reach this point, from the first time humanoids walked the earth – approximately 200,000 years ago – to the beginning of the 19th century! Since then the population has grown with lightning speed. For the second billion we needed hardly more than a century. Queen Victoria of the United Kingdom (who reigned from 1837-1901) lived through what amounted to the doubling of the human population in her lifetime. When Roger Moore was born in 1927, the world had two billion inhabitants. When he played James Bond for the first time in *Live and Let Die* in 1973, the population of the world had already doubled again to four billion. When he played the role of the famed MI6 agent for the last time in *A View to a Kill* in 1985, there were nearly a billion more. In short: the first billion took humanity a couple of hundred thousand years, while the leap from four billion to five billion went as fast as the James Bond career of a well-known British actor.

Today, there are approximately seven billion people and according to the most recent estimates of the United Nations, the population of the world will probably have stabilized around 2100. At that point, it should be around 11 billion.

Around the time of the first spectacular growth of the population in the 18th century, the first prophets of doom also turned up, predicting that the sharp increase in population would become a threat to food supply, peace and the planet. The forefather of this school of pessimists is Thomas Malthus. In 1798 he published *An Essay on the Principle of Population*. In it he proposes that the growth of a population follows an exponential path: two parents have four children. Those four children will have given birth to a total of 16 children, and a generation later those 16 children will together have 64 children between them. During a better part of human history, near-zero growth was the norm, and an exponential increase in the population was a new phenomenon at the time. Since the start of the industrial revolution, child mortality had been declining, allowing the population to grow at a particularly rapid rate (see illustration 15).

Illustration 15: **Billions and milestones**
Sources: United Nations (1999), *The World at Six Billion*,
United Nations (2004) *World Population to 2300*,
United States Census Bureau http://www.prb.org/Articles/2002/
HowManyPeopleHaveEverLIvedonEarth.aspx,
United Nations (2013), *World Population Prospects*, the 2012 revision

Billion	Date	Number of years needed	Average annual growth
1	1804	entire human history	almost zero
2	1927	123	0.6
3	1960	33	1.2
4	1974	14	2.1
5	1987	13	1.7
6	1999	12	1.5
7	2012	13	1.2
8	2024	12	1.1
9	2040	16	0.7
10	2062	22	0.5

At the same time, Malthus proposes that food production follows a linear path. The total agricultural or food production can, according to him, be increased, but will never be able to catch up with the explosive growth of the population. His analysis and prediction was thus clear: an exploding population in combination with slow-growing food production will lead to famine, conflicts or food wars. These are according to him natural phenomena as well: a necessary evil that ensures that a population will again shrink to a level in keeping with available agricultural production through disease, deprivation or war.

Limiting population growth was in Malthus's view the only remedy that would save mankind from certain decline. Helping the poor or bettering their circumstances was in his opinion imprudent. Better living conditions would simply lead to the impoverished population bearing more children, which would only hasten the impending famine. If Malthus were alive today, would he think the West completely irresponsible for helping developing countries to raise their standard of living or for trying to reduce child mortality?

It is precisely this deeply cynical reasoning that is defended by the contemporary environmental philosopher Garrett Hardin. He is not only known for *The tragedy of the commons* (see chapter 4), but is also the author of *Living on a Lifeboat*. Like his guru Malthus, he emphasizes the impending problem of overpopulation. In the 1974 article he rejects the metaphor of 'the earth as a spaceship'. In that view, we all share the earth, and the fate of the entire population of the world is ultimately interdependent. The strongest therefore have a moral duty to help the weakest. This is not how the world looks according to Hardin. He prefers the metaphor of a lifeboat: when wealthy Westerners try to save as many poor drowning victims as possible, the lifeboat Earth will inevitably sink. In his view, high birth rates in the third world are just another reason not to lend a helping hand. It would only encourage them to produce more children and, in this way, exacerbate the problem of overpopulation. The high mortality of the third world is, in his view, just another natural way to restore the balance between population growth and food supply.

Not only is he an opponent of giving food aid to poor countries, he also wants to limit migration for the same reasons. Migration is for him nothing short of 'inverted food aid': the poor come to the food instead of the other way around.

Malthusians continue to turn up like clockwork right up to the present. Their scheme is always the same: every one of them emphasizes the limited possibilities of expanding available natural resources and the near exponential growth of human needs. The human being is a parasite that threatens to make the earth uninhabitable. The initial focus was primarily on the degree to which a growing human population placed untenable pressure on available agricultural ground. The more evident it became that the 'Great Famine' was not just around the corner, the more frequently the Malthusians began to point out the finite supply of other natural resources: from coal to oil and from copper to aluminum. Certainly an environment in which the world population increases by approximately one billion every decade and a half gives the Malthusians grist to the mill. Below are a few recent examples of Malthusian prophets of doom:

» In 1865 – in the middle of the industrial revolution – the British economist William Stanley Jevons wrote *The Coal Question*. In it he discussed the possible exhaustion of coal as fuel for industry, the economy and wealth. The headlong rush of economic and industrial activity would lead to the end of existing coal supplies and cause growth to come to an abrupt halt.

» The American geophysicist Marion King Hubbert produced a variation on the same theme. In 1956, when he worked for the Shell research lab, he described how worldwide oil production would reach its apex sooner rather than later – *Peak Oil* – only to decrease until existing oil supplies were completely exhausted.

This theory not only made a big impression on public opinion at the time, it also helped shape the energy policy of the United States to a significant degree. With political and geopolitical consequences that still resonate to this day.

» The American professor Paul Ehrlich published his much talked-about book *The Population Bomb* in 1968. In it he predicted the mass starvation and death of hundreds of millions of people from the 1970s onward through a combination of an exploding world population and insufficient food production. He had a number of radical solutions in mind to drastically reduce the growth of the world population, such as mandatory sterilization, a tax on children and a luxury tax on childcare products. Reserving food aid for developing countries with a low birth rate also seemed like a good idea to him. In that way, he thought the growth of the world population could be stanched.

» In 1972 the Club of Rome published the paper *Limits to Growth*. They too drew on the old familiar Malthusian recipe: uncontrolled population growth and finite natural resources would cause the earth to implode and pitch us into economic disaster. The Club made detailed calculations of how long it would take before the various available natural resources were permanently exhausted. Its paper remains for many Malthusians the definitive reference for arguing in favor of zero growth for the economy or the population.

The reasoning of contemporary Malthusians is easy to sum up: "Ten billion people times an American lifestyle equals an ecological and economic disaster." Even today, there is an abundance of gurus, authors, organizations and pressure groups that continue to point to the irreconcilability of economic growth or population growth on the one side and an inhabitable planet on the other. Nevertheless, their theories – in several versions – were always overtaken by the facts in the past. And always because of the same flaws in their reasoning.

In particular, the Malthusians underestimate human ingenuity and humanity's immense capacity for innovation in order to adapt to the natural environment. The growth of the population and human needs is perfectly visible, demonstrable in numbers and comes across as threatening. Belching smokestacks, cities bursting at the seams, underfed African children, overfed American children, comparisons of ecological footprints and images of failed harvests in developing countries belong to the standard arsenal of arguments and image-building intended to sow unrest concerning the inhabitability of the planet. The countless scientists who today work on the technologies of the future, the crops of the future, the car of the future, the energy of the future and the cities of the future are much less frequently depicted. Their invention, and future developments in technology and science that will take on human, technological or environmental challenges, are not yet visible.

Since the prophecy of Thomas Malthus, the population of the world has increased more than sevenfold (see illustration 16). At the same time, life expectancy and the average income have risen significantly, while child mortality and poverty have dropped dramatically. The ability of humankind to adapt to its environment is thus consistently greater than the pessimists thought possible. Nothing suggests that that will no longer be the case in the future. The burden of proof lies with the Malthusians: they must argue against the overwhelming proof of the past two centuries, in which humankind has surmounted all major challenges.

Malthus, Jevons, Hubbert, Ehrlich and the Club of Rome were each and every one overtaken by reality. They went too far in their conclusions that finite resources could not be combined with a growing world population, human needs, and economic activity. The mass mortality and food shortage wars that were predicted by Malthus, Ehrlich and Hardin never arrived in the end. The use of artificial fertilizers, mechanization of agriculture, better irrigation, genetic modification and cross-pollination of crops ensured a spectacular increase in both the yield and production volume of cultivated crops.

Just when the peak in coal production predicted by Jevons was reached, oil became the most widely used industrial fuel. The coal supply was indeed finite, but not human ingenuity: we changed over to a more efficient, cheaper alternative. The same goes for Hubbert's *Peak Oil* theory. While the output of conventional oil sources today does indeed reach the level of the production peak, more and more alternative sources are being discovered and exploited. The increasing scarcity of conventional oil sent oil prices skyrocketing and made the exploitation of other sources in difficult locations – shale gas and oil, for example – suddenly profitable. Necessity is the mother of invention. And the free market and price mechanism are the catalysts needed to make that necessity felt.

THE POWER OF IMAGINATION

Malthusians doe not take into account the power of innovation. They primarily take limited production capacity as their point of departure. The optimists, by contrast, take the unbounded inventiveness of the human imagination as their point of departure. Or, in other words: improvements in productivity. These represent the only real increase in human welfare. Welfare is not only measured on the basis of production processes, traffic, transport, communication and healthcare. Throughout the history of countless countries, a structural improvement of living standards has always begun with an increase in agricultural production. Small-scale, rudimentary and low-tech agriculture on small plots of land is what kept people poor, sick, miserable, and stagnant for millennia. It was intensive cultivation on larger plots, with better technology and greater productivity that saved us from the Malthusian famine. It has always been human ingenuity and ambition for a better life that have made the difference. Every one of the examples below proves that Malthus and his followers were wrong.

» At the end of the 19th century, a Dutch milk cow gave around 1,900 liters of milk per year. By 1950, that figure had already risen to 3,300 liters and in 2000 had reached a level of more than 8,000 liters per year. The average ecological footprint per liter of milk produced has also declined spectacularly. The emission of phosphorous, carbon monoxide and ammonia per hectare today is around half the level it was 40 years ago. The most important causes of this progress are to be found in better feed, better business practices and genetic selection of the cows.

» In chicken farming, too, the profitability of production has risen sharply. A chicken raised using intensive farming techniques takes six weeks from egg to slaughterhouse before entering the food chain. The animals are raised in cages and hardly see the

Illustration 16: **Malthus and friends**
Sources: Lee (2003), *The Demographic Transition: Three Centuries of Fundamental Change*, UN World Population Prospects, 2012 revision, United States Census Bureau

Author	Prophecy	Year	World population	Growth*
		1700	680 million	0.5%
Malthus	*Essay on the Principle of Population*	1798	980 million	0.5%
Paul Ehrlich	*The Population Bomb*	1968	3.56 billion	2.2%
Club of Rome	*Limits to growth*	1972	3.86 billion	2.1%
Garett Hardin	*Living on a Lifeboat*	1974	4.00 billion	2.1%
		2012	7 billion	1.1%
		2062	10 billion	0.5%

* Average annual growth

111

light of day. Bio-chickens, by contrast, take around 28 days longer to reach adulthood and roam freely in the open air.

In public opinion, intensive poultry farming and the broilers it produces can hardly expect sympathy. The bio-chicken seems like a paragon of sustainability by comparison. But appearances can be deceiving: the ecological footprint of a bio-chicken is nearly 75% higher than that of a broiler. Professor Dijkhuizen of the University of Wageningen states that it is an illusion to think that 'bio' is synonymous with a better planet. A bio-chicken has to be fed longer, produces more ammonia, converts food less efficiently into meat and needs a lot more time to mature. According to Dutch calculations, the total ecological footprint of a broiler is approximately 3.3 kilograms of greenhouse gas per kilogram of meat, as opposed to at least 5.2 kilograms of greenhouse gas per bio-chicken. Given a total chicken production in the Netherlands of around a half a billion (in 2010), this makes a world of difference.

Illustration 17: **Agricultural yield for corn**
Source: World Bank, *Rising Global Interest in Farmland* (2011)

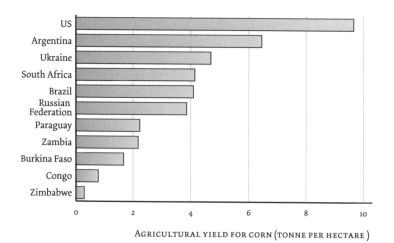

AGRICULTURAL YIELD FOR CORN (TONNE PER HECTARE)

» In agricultural production generally there is also a great deal of profit to be gained by efficiency. Let us examine the figures from the World Bank for corn production worldwide (see illustration 17). From one hectare of corn, a country like Zimbabwe harvests a mere 300 kilograms. Neighboring Zambia sees a yield that is seven times as high. South Africa is the African record holder and succeeds in producing 4.1 tons of corn per hectare. The United States, however, wins the productivity prize: they harvest at least 9.7 tons of corn per hectare. Imagine what would happen if the agricultural yield of the United States dropped back to the level of Zimbabwe's – it is clear that the country would never be able to equal its level of corn production today. Better yet: even if the United States planted corn on every square centimeter of ground, its total production would be less than what it is now. Small-scale agriculture makes it impossible to feed a larger population – this is the experience of human history. Particularly in developing countries, the potential for yield improvements is still enormous. Many countries now produce only 20% of what would be possible on the same surface area using current techniques and technology. In other words: if those countries changed over to the newest production techniques and engaged in more intensive agriculture, they would be able to increase their production at least fivefold.

» The average size of an agricultural concern plays an important role in productivity. An average American agricultural concern is nearly 180 hectares, as opposed to 32 hectares in Europe and less than three in sub-Saharan Africa. For a large agricultural concern, mechanization is a must, so that productivity can be increased automatically. For someone with a small parcel of only two hectares, the purchase of a tractor, agricultural machine or crop duster is not profitable, which further cuts down on growth and productivity. Potential improvements to productivity in underdeveloped areas can help us a great deal in meeting the challenges of a greater population. Higher productivity has many faces: mechanized agriculture, fertilizers, genetic techniques, rational water use.

» In the agricultural sector, it is also necessary to improve the yield of seeds by making them more resistant to disease and drought. Among other things, the use of genetically improved crops can make a significant contribution to this goal. It is not by chance that a scientist like Norman Borlaug won the Nobel Peace Prize in 1970 for the genetic manipulation of wheat varieties. Thanks to his research, nearly a billion people were saved from starvation. Borlaug's work is a perfect example of how innovation and increased productivity are an answer to one of the greatest challenges facing humanity. For this reason alone you could call him an anti-Malthus.

» Necessity is the mother of invention – and not only in agriculture. The increase in oil prices in recent decades has also brought about a strong increase in the efficiency of road transport. The first two *cheveux* by Citroën weighed approximately 500 kilograms, delivered 1 horsepower, reached a top speed of 65 kilometers per hour, and used 4.4 liters of fuel per 100 kilometers. Citroën's smallest model today is the C_1. It weighs around 800 kilograms, delivers 64 horsepower, reaches a top speed of around 160 kilometers per hour, and uses 4.6 liters per 100 kilometers. In other words: the same amount of fuel displaces more weight, reaches a higher maximum speed, and delivers more power. The efficiency of the available source of strength has thus increased spectacularly. The fact that the total gasoline consumption of the car has remained more or less the same, on the other hand, means that the gain in efficiency has been converted entirely into extra comfort: better seats, air-conditioning, ABS, airbags, security bars, and a more attractive, solid interior. A car that weighs as much as the original two-cylinder would hardly use any fuel at all. Lighter yet safer materials are also a possible solution to making cars more efficient.

The second central tenet of the Malthusians is that the population explosion will inevitably continue until it ends in civil war or food conflicts. Here too the claim appears to be highly exaggerated. The world population today is primarily undergoing a 'demographic transition': from a small but rapidly growing population to a large but stagnating population.

Whether we are talking about a city, a country, a continent or even the whole world, population growth can always be reduced to the relationship between two numbers: the birth rate and the death rate. The difference between these two is population growth, whether it is positive or negative. As long as the birth rate and death rate are approximately the same, the population stabilizes and is stationary. For most of human history this was the case: a sky-high birth rate in combination with a sky-high death rate. This was the first phase of the demographic transition. In illustration 18 it is shown at the

Illustration 18: **The demographic transition**

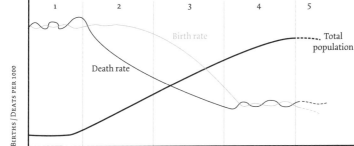

115

far left. The red line shows the development of the total population: it is fairly constant. The population pyramid shows the relationship between different population groups in society. The very youngest are at the bottom, and the higher up the pyramid we go, the greater the age. In the first phase, the population pyramid has the typical form of a dented Christmas tree. There are many, many young people (high birth rate) in relation to very few old people (high death rate).

The second phase is the early growth phase. Thanks to better healthcare, better hygiene and more general knowledge among the population, the death rate has gone down considerably. Not so much because people are suddenly growing very old, but because of the spectacular drop in child mortality. Initially the birth rate remains fairly high for cultural reasons. That is: because tradition demands that women have many children and because family planning is taboo, still more children survive their fifth birthdays than in the past. The result is that the population shoots up dramatically. The population pyramid at this point resembles a fully formed Christmas tree. This is a society in which the number of young people has increased very quickly in a very short time. This has the requisite consequences for the political stability of the country in question (see the box "Christmas trees are dangerous, glass-recycling bins are not"). The strong population growth of the last few decades (see illustration 15) can be largely explained by the dramatic reduction of the death rate among children (see illustrations 19 and 20). The apparently bad news (an exploding population) is thus the result of very good news (lower child mortality). The population explosion in itself is no reason for panic: for many poor countries it is the effect of a healthier and better life that has led to lower child mortality. The primary effect of decreasing child mortality is also an exploding population. The secondary effect is a decrease in the birth rate. Healthier children and lower child mortality reduce the need for a high number of births per woman. And we need this lower birth rate in order to reach the next phase.

The third phase is the late growth phase or the near-stationary phase. The death rate is still decreasing, but much less spectacularly than in the second phase. More important is that from this moment, the birth rate also begins to decrease. Improved living conditions and improvements in agricultural productivity mean that families no longer need to have a lot of children. Children are no longer tools that can be put to work in the fields. On the contrary, by sending them to school, they form an investment in the future. Notice that this is the opposite of what Malthus and his followers claim: they saw better living conditions as a source of even more children instead of what we find in practice: increased liberation of women and family planning cause the birth rate to decline. Nevertheless, the population continues to grow in the third phase: the birth rate is still higher than the death rate. The population pyramid looks less like a pyramid and begins to look more like a bell. This is a population in which young people are no longer the dominant group. Society's attention shifts from saving young lives to prolonging existing lives. Adult life expectancy increases and the number of old people slowly increases.

At the extreme end of the demographic transition we end up once more in a stationary phase. The birth rate has at that moment decreased even further, until it is close to an already very low death rate. Today, we find this situation in Japan or Europe, for example. In the first phase of the demographic transition the population stagnated as a result of a sky-high birth rate in combination with an equally high death rate. In the last phase, the population stagnates through a combination of a low birth rate and a low death rate. Sometimes the birth rate will decrease even further, with a shrinking population as a result. The population pyramid in this phase looks more and more like a glass recycling bin: the youngest generation is less numerous than the generation just above it. These are also societies in which old people form a substantial part of the population and in which those old people control society in all possible ways: economically, financially and politically. These are stable societies, both politically and socially: a relatively high median age, attached to the status quo, less innovative than young societies, and not interested in radical social experiments.

The different nations of the world now find themselves in different stages of the demographic transition. Some African countries are still in the second phase, while countries like Germany or Japan already seem to have passed the fourth phase and are shrinking. The world as a whole presently finds itself somewhere between the second and third phase. There is nothing to indicate that the world will remain there indefinitely and that the population will continue growing as fast as a runaway freight train. In many former developing countries, for example, the birth rate in recent decades is already decreasing significantly. It is also expected that most countries will slowly pass through the various stages in the decades to come. At that point the world as a whole will start evolving towards stabilization of the total population in the years to come. According to estimates of the United Nations, the world population will stagnate around the year 2100 at approximately 11 billion inhabitants.

Illustration 19: **Child mortality historically low**
Source: www.gapminder.org

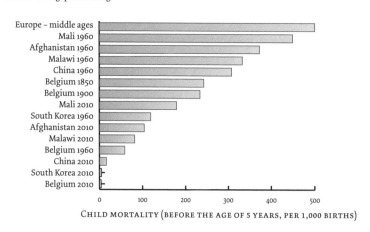

CHILD MORTALITY (BEFORE THE AGE OF 5 YEARS, PER 1,000 BIRTHS)

Although this seems like a gigantic figure, it should be seen in perspective. Because it is difficult to form a concrete image of such figures, imagine that the entire world population of 11 billion people moved to Australia. In other words: a megalopolis on the Australian continent. There would be approximately 1,400 people per square kilometer. This is more or less the present population density of a city like Mechelen – where life seems to be good – but then the size of Australia. The good news is that the remaining 95% of the landmass worldwide would be completely uninhabited. But perhaps not everybody likes living in cities. That's quite possible. Nevertheless it seems to be, increasingly, humanity's preference. Today, for the first time in history, more than half of the world's inhabitants live in cities. By 2030, that will even have increased to more than 60%.

Illustration 20: **Child mortality in free fall**
Source: Unicef, Report on Child Mortality (2012)

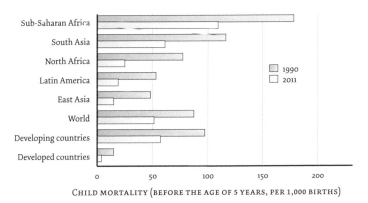

CHILD MORTALITY (BEFORE THE AGE OF 5 YEARS, PER 1,000 BIRTHS)

The demographic transition is not only important for interpreting the current and expected growth of the world population. It can also be used as an explanation for the lack of political or military instability in particular countries or regions. The term most often used in this context is 'youth bulge'. Although a 'youth surplus' is a fairly literal definition, it would be more accurate to speak of a 'boy surplus'. The theory of the youth surplus has gained in importance over the past few years. Briefly summarized, it amounts to the following: A rapidly growing population – from phase two – is characterized by extremely fast growth of the number of young people in society. This surplus of young people – in particular boys – often causes great tension. In families in which the eldest or eldest two sons inherit, the younger sons will feel they have been marginalized. For this reason, their chances on the job market are also limited. In an earlier era, they might not have survived their fifth birthdays, but thanks to the decrease in child mortality they have grown into young adults. A sudden increase in the number of young people is also frequently paired with sky-high youth unemployment. In contemporary developing countries, it is often three to five times higher among young people than among the rest of the total population. The weak financial and economic position of boys, moreover, lowers their position with respect to a future marriage. Add to that the typical impulsiveness of male adolescents in combination with one radical ideology or another, and it is immediately clear that a surplus of boys can easily become a security risk.

A number of studies show that a large proportion of young people between 16 and 30 – the so-called fighting age – significantly increases the chance of unrest or civil war. Wars are, after all, fought by 18-year-old boys without possessions or status, not by 45-year-old men with families, social position and property. Illustration 21 shows the link between the proportion of youth in a society and the chance of armed conflict. Each point represents a period of civil war or armed conflict, each time arranged along two axes: the vertical shows youth as a percentage of the total population; the horizontal, older people as a percentage of the population. The gray line shows the relationship between both groups throughout different phases of the demographic transition. From this graph it is evident that conflicts are substantially more frequent in 'young' and rapidly growing societies than in 'old' societies.

The critical boundary is reached when more than 60% of the population is younger than 30. Such societies have a much greater risk of armed conflict. For this reason they also have little chance of developing into liberal democracies. In illustration 21, civil wars or armed conflicts are represented by the small colored squares. On both axes, they show what proportion of society as a whole is made up of young and old people, respectively. At the upper left we find the 'youngest' populations and the most armed conflicts. At the lower right we find the oldest populations and almost no armed conflict. Young populations are clearly associated with more violence and less stability.

Illustration 21: **Boy surplus and civil war**
Source: Cincotta and Leahy (2007), *Population age structure and its relation to civil conflict: a graphic metric*, ECSP Report n°12.

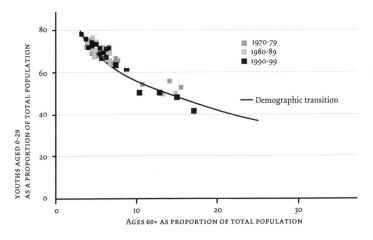

In the 1990s, for example, countries with more than 45 births per 1,000 inhabitants had more than one chance in two of experiencing an armed conflict. In countries with a birth rate of between 15 and 25 per 1,000 inhabitants, that risk dropped to only 16%. Fewer births mean less violence. Greater military or geopolitical stability in the world has much less to do with reforms, human rights, democratization or the holding of free elections than we would like to think. Although every one of these is a necessary condition for a stable society, real change starts from within the population pyramid: a democratic transition demands a demographic transition. Europe is at the very end of the demographic transition: an old population that will soon be shrinking, and an age pyramid that resembles a fat glass-recycling bin. Many countries in Africa or the Middle East are just beginning to make the transition: these are countries with a population pyramid that looks like a small, cramped Christmas tree.

Europe itself has been through the demographic transition. In European history, periods of civil unrest were often preceded by a very strong increase in the population. The conclusion is the same each time: an overdose of young people/boys results in dangerous conditions and stunts democracy.

A decreasing birth rate is thus not only crucial for the stabilization of the world population, but also for a safer society. In nearly all regions in the world, the birth rate has been declining for some time. One religion is not more violent than another. One continent is not more warlike than another. Age pyramids, population structures, birth rates and death rates, however, do differ strongly worldwide. There are demographically 'unsafe' regions, for example, such as the Middle East or sub-Saharan Africa. The population is growing explosively there thanks to a decrease in the death rate that has not yet been followed by a decrease in the birth rate. With a gigantic proportion of youth at fighting age, it is especially difficult to build a stable, functioning society – let alone a democracy. Conflict, violence, and war will still be the scourge of these countries for some time. There, too, every democratic transition will begin with a demographic transition. This often coincides with an improvement of the position of women. Studies show that lower birth rates are in fact the result of a consistent policy of ensuring the literacy and education of girls (that is, the future mothers). The literacy, education and emancipation of women are probably the best strategies for reducing child mortality in the first place, and the birth rate in the second. Women are thus the key to a lower birth rate and a successful demographic transition.

At the opposite end of the spectrum we find Europe and Japan. The median age is high, there is a shortage of young people and the population hardly grows at all. These are not countries that will quickly end up in an armed conflict today. They are old, getting older and no longer need war to die out slowly.

The good news is that the population structure on a world level is always getting 'safer'. The bad news is that there are still many countries with an overdose of young people. They will remain geopolitical hotspots for some time to come. The list is still fairly long and contains all the usual suspects: Congo, Pakistan, Afghanistan, Iran, Iraq, Palestine... The prescription for a safer world in the long run is thus also quite simple: get more girls in school, set the Christmas tree out on the curb and install a glass-recycling bin at home.

THE FUTURE: MORE PEOPLE AND EVEN MORE INNOVATION

Things will turn out all right with that supposedly unbridled, all-destroying growth of the world population. First and foremost, the population explosion of the past century is primarily a sign that things are going well for the human race. Health is improving, death rates and birth rates are decreasing and affluence is on the rise. The population explosion is also a health explosion. Although all those billions are quite impressive, this period of mass population growth is a temporary phenomenon. We are all going through a demographic transition that within a century or so – perhaps even this century – should result in the stabilization of the world population.

In the meantime, many are breaking out in a cold sweat whenever they think of the 'humanity of ten billion'. The modern Malthusians will leave no stone unturned to present humanity as a threat to the planet and to itself. Humanity that pollutes itself sick, destroys its environment and lays waste to the earth. The pessimism of the Malthusians is a barely concealed form of misanthropy. Their talk of ecological footprints, carbon-kilometers and apocalyptic predictions of an imploding climate are constantly presenting us with an image of humanity as a plague upon the earth.

At heart, the Malthusians simply don't believe in people. They certainly don't believe in innovation. They don't believe in people's capacity to make their environment a better place. They see people not as saviors of the planet, but as its greatest threat. They would prefer to pull all the strings themselves and conduct the behavior of individual citizens in the direction of what they think will be a better world. "People don't know what's good for them, but we do..."

And here they are sadly mistaken. The experience of the past two centuries is the best proof that humanity is continually progressing on nearly all levels. People are not the problem, but the solution. Give a person a challenge, and all the freedom in the world to take it on, and he or she will emerge victorious. In a system of free markets, prices will alert people to the fact of scarcity. In the first place, this will cause consumer behavior to change. We consume less of what becomes more expensive. Whether it's open space, oil, environmental pollution, CO_2 emissions or raw materials.

The second effect is perhaps even more pronounced: higher prices set the human inclination toward innovation in motion. This allows people to go in search of more efficient, cheaper or better ways to interact with their environment. Decreeing in advance what the right production technique or the best fuel will be, or what foods we may or may not eat, shows a strange sort of belief in an all-knowing, all-powerful government. It is striking to see how people with an almost religious faith in such an all-knowing government as the solution for all problems are often the same people who consistently distrust large corporations on account of the same alleged omnipotence.

"Innovation and technology as a source of progress" is not just a naïve belief; it is a brief summary of the past two centuries of human history and progress. It is also only from them that our future affluence will come. The inventions that will radically change our lives the day after tomorrow still have to be invented tomorrow. Perhaps within 50 years we will print out our steak and vegetables on the basis of the carbon produced by our energy production. Perhaps we will use the same printer to make donor organs. Perhaps we will cultivate genetically altered bananas or rice in which a vaccine for malaria or aids has been incorporated on a scale large enough to feed the world. Perhaps we will finally make nuclear fusion operational. Perhaps we will invent teleportation. Perhaps by then we will have a colony on Mars. Whatever may be, technology and innovation are the keys to greater affluence, more wealth. Humanity itself will prove Malthus and all his followers wrong. Simply by doing what it has already done for centuries: using a combination of better technologies and altered behaviors, adapting to the challenging natural environment.

CHAPTER 8

Everybody unemployed

"The production of too many useful things results in too many useless people." — **Karl Marx**

"Any existing structures and all the conditions of doing business are always in a process of change. Every situation is being upset before it has had time to work itself out. Economic progress, in a capitalist society, means turmoil."
— **Joseph Schumpeter**, Austrian economist (1883-1950)

"As a matter of fact, capitalist economy is not and cannot be stationary. Nor is it merely expanding in a steady manner. It is incessantly being revolutionized from within by new enterprise, i.e., by the intrusion of new commodities or new methods of production or new commercial opportunities into the industrial structure as it exists at any moment."
— **Joseph Schumpeter**

"Leverage is a glimpse of prosperity you haven't really earned." — **Michael Lewis**, American author and financial journalist (°1960)

Ned Ludd was an English weaver from Leicester area who lived at the end of the 18th century – in the midst of the industrial revolution, that is. At one point he tried to turn back progress by smashing a number of mechanized looms to pieces. Today, looms have pretty much become the symbol of the industrial revolution. For Ned Ludd they were also the primary cause of rising unemployment. Against a background of poverty and deprivation brought about by the Napoleonic wars, the large-scale introduction of mechanized looms ensured that suddenly there were far fewer workers needed. Through mechanization, the same amount of fabric could be woven using the effort of far fewer people. Automated looms were, for Ned Ludd, not a symbol of economic progress, but rather of social decline. In subsequent years others followed his example: in a number of locations around England, looms and other machines were destroyed. Although the vandals were by no means part of a well-defined organization, this movement is still known to this day under the rubric of 'Luddism'. Even all these years after the industrial revolution, there are still 'Luddites' today. Although the Malthusians do not believe in

Illustration 22:
Twenty years of innovation
Source: Mind Blowing Facts
(Twitter)

progress through technological innovation (see chapter 7), Luddites see innovation as a threat to employment opportunities and 'the old way of life'.

NEW TECHNOLOGY IS ALWAYS DISRUPTIVE

New technology, new production techniques and innovations are often disruptive and controversial. They often lead to major social, economic and financial revolutions. The development of the steamboat meant the end of the sailing ship as a means of mass transportation. The telegraph was made superfluous by the invention of the telephone. Artificial substances replaced wood and metal, the icebox made the milkman redundant and e-mail has (more or less) meant the end of posted letters.

A recent and highly recognizable example of disruptive technology is the iPhone by Apple – shown in illustration 22. The two photos are separated by barely 20 years of progress and innovation. The iPhone takes up less space, provides better quality services, is easier to assemble and use, and moreover, uses far less raw materials and energy than all of its predecessors put together. Also important to mention: the innovation and progress between the two photos was not imposed, forced or decreed. There was no government call for tenders "for the replacement of the camera, Walkman, calculator, postal service, portable phone, portable computer and watch by one new application." The iPhone exists because a private firm wanted to make a profit by innovating. This kind of disruptive innovation – a negative shock for old industries, a positive shock for wealth – does not come about by government decree. They are here thanks to the free market, which ensures competition. They are here thanks to competition, which keeps companies on their toes and drives them to innovate.

The combination of telephone, music library, e-mail, digital camera and pocket computer – the iPhone, in effect – was nothing short of catastrophic for many traditional companies and enterprises: producers of vinyl records or CDs, record shops, postal concerns, producers of film rolls, Polaroid cameras, office calculators, GPS devices and fixed-line telephones. For profitability and employment in their sector, the iPhone was an absolute disaster.

This is the 'paradox of progress'. New technologies and innovation largely generate progress and higher living standards for everyone, but the initial and most immediate effect is that existing industries encounter difficulties, lose profits and sometimes disappear entirely. The increase in wealth is only visible in the long run; in the short run it is primarily the negative consequences that predominate: specific employees in specific industries lose their jobs as a result of competition, innovation and new technology. Furniture companies that disappear after the arrival of IKEA. The milkman who loses his job because everyone has a refrigerator. Small, local sports shops that disappear after the introduction of giants like Decathlon or online sporting goods stores. Bookstores that take a beating from the iBookstore or Amazon. Ryanair and easyJet, whose innovative business models make life hard for classic airline companies. The losers of the contest of competition and innovation see new technologies, new entrepreneurs and new business models primarily as negative. This is why progress is often initially perceived as decline.

IMPACT ON THE JOB MARKET

Job destruction and job creation are the yin and yang of a rising prosperity. Without destruction, creation is not possible. Without creation, destruction is not possible. Adam Smith also described this phenomenon in his 1776 *Wealth of Nations*. Smith used the now-famous example of the safety-pin factory. An individual laborer could make a maximum of 20 safety pins per day "without the help of machines." With the help of machines and an efficient division of labor, he could produce at least 4,800 per day. In other words: before the introduction of machines, a factory with 240 workers had a daily output of 4,800 safety pins. After mechanization, at least 239 people would lose their jobs, while production would remain the same. One might call it a spectacular increase in unemployment and an apparent decrease in wealth. Nevertheless, the opposite is true.

The introduction of new technology makes a number of existing jobs superfluous and causes unemployment. On the other hand, new technology will ensure the creation of new jobs and new ways of creating wealth. Before the development of the steam engine, the ships that plied our inland waterways were drawn by humans or horses. With the development of the steam engine, towing barges disappeared and were replaced by steamships. The immediate consequence was unemployment among those who used to drag the ships or drive the horses. Thanks to the steamships, however, there were new jobs, some of which didn't even exist before: people were needed to transport coal, man the steam engine and maintain the engine.

Individually, the new technology resulted in winners and losers. Collectively, wealth increased and society as a whole progressed. And this is still true today. But that does not mean the whole process takes place painlessly. Behind the structural increase in wealth are hidden numerous individual dramas among those groups of people who lose their jobs in the name of progress. Not so long ago the American Central Bank made a survey of American job destruction and creation in the 21st century (see illustration 23). It was immediately clear that creation and destruction together are a continuous and extensive phenomenon. In 1910, there were still more than 11 million Americans who worked in agriculture out of an American population that at the time counted less than 100 million people. At the beginning of the 1990s, less than one million Americans worked in agriculture, although the population had in the meantime grown to around 250 million. Freight truck, bus and taxi drivers did not exist at the beginning of the 20th century. At the end of the century there were more than three million.

Of course, illustration 23 shows primarily the most striking examples of destruction and creation. Those who interpret the illustration literally and deduct all the jobs destroyed from the jobs created might get the impression that there is a net loss of jobs. This is anything but the case. In 1900, the population of America was around 76 million people, of which approximately 30 million were employed. In 2013, the American population has grown to around 250 million and at least 140 million of them have jobs. Not only are there around five times as many people working today than at the beginning of the 20th century, the number of those employed has also grown in proportion to the population. In spite of job destruction. Thanks to job creation.

In Belgium things were no different: old sectors disappeared and new sectors appeared. A hundred years ago, agriculture was pretty much the largest employer in Belgium. At the same time, no one worked in computer science, airplane manufacture, fitness centers, petrochemicals, nanotechnology, airports, nuclear power plants, solar panels, fair trade, computer sales, web design, food safety, management consulting, space travel, TV production, developing apps, chemical production, cancer research, laser technology, or biotechnology. The continual process of old sectors disappearing and new sectors appearing is also known as *creative destruction*. It is the quintessential combination of near-contemporaneous destruction and creation that is crucial for increasing wealth. The process itself can be painful at times; the result is an increase in living standards.

Today there are still Luddites among us who resist progress and fight the disappearance of certain industries. Auto manufacturing, the textile industry, and the steel sector come to mind. It would be senseless to try and hold back the processes of creative destruction. Prolonging the lifetime of disappearing industries longer than necessary impedes the development of emerging industries or the sectors of the future. It is only by allowing destruction that the creation of new industries and more wealth becomes possible. Of course, in such cases provisions should be made for assisting those whose industries or sectors are affected by destruction. What is advantageous to society as a whole can sometimes be extremely painful for a limited group of employees. Therefore it is important to invest in the

Illustration 23: **Destruction and creation**
Source: Federal Reserve Bank of Dallas (1992)

	People employed		
Destruction	**Today**	**Yesterday**	
Railroad employees	231,000	2,076,000	1920
Carriage and harness makers	*	109,000	1900
Telegraph operators	8,000	75,000	1920
Boilermakers	*	74,000	1920
Milliners	*	100,000	1910
Cobblers	25,000	102,000	1900
Blacksmiths	*	238,000	1910
Watchmakers	*	101,000	1920
Switchboard operators	213,000	421,000	1970
Farm workers	851,000	11,533,000	1910
Creation	**Today**	**Yesterday**	
Airline pilots and mechanics	232,000	0	1900
Medical technicians	1,379,000	0	1910
Engineers	1,846,000	38,000	1900
Computer programmers /operators	1,287,000	*	1960
Fax machine workers	699,000	0	1980
Auto mechanics	864,000		1900
Truck-, bus and taxi drivers	3,328,000	0	1900
Professional athletes	77,000	*	1920
TV and radio announcers	60,000	*	1930
Electricians/electronic repairers	711,000	51,000	1900
Optometrists	62,000	*	1910

* Less than 5,000

efficiency and flexibility of employees and those who seek employment: mobility, training and internships are all essential in streamlining the process of getting people in place for new opportunities.

MAXIMUM WEALTH OR MAXIMUM EMPLOYMENT?

Old sectors disappear and new sectors appear. That is the recipe for progress and increasing wealth. By extension, old jobs disappear and new jobs appear. What is the net balance of jobs? Do more jobs appear than disappear, or vice versa? This is an extremely important question, especially for political purposes. Politicians and central bankers often speak of goals such as 'total employment'. When they do, they give the impression that the goal is to get everyone between the ages of 15 and 65 working. This goal is neither attainable nor desirable, however, and it is contradicted by the experience of the past few centuries. The economy, and by extension economic

Illustration 24: **We work less and less**
Source: International Labour organisation(2007), *Working time around the world*

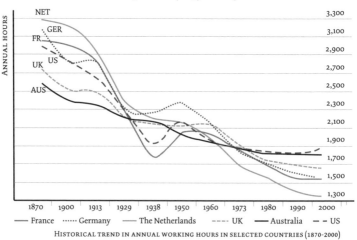

HISTORICAL TREND IN ANNUAL WORKING HOURS IN SELECTED COUNTRIES (1870-2000)

134

growth, is a means for ensuring maximum social progress, not maximum employment. Employment and wealth are two different concepts.

To the extent that we have all become wealthier – collectively and individually, in Belgium, Europe and the West – we have devoted a large portion of that wealth to more leisure and less work (see illustration 24). The workweek and careers have become shorter; leisure time and retirement have become longer. When universal retirement benefits were introduced in Belgium, the average life expectancy was lower than the legal retirement age. Retirement benefits at that time were more of an insurance policy for those who had the misfortune to live beyond the age of 65. Today, not only is the effective retirement age in Belgium lower than 60, but people also enjoy their retirement benefits for more than 20 years on average. Not only do people live longer, they also spend a greater percentage of their lives in good health. At the end of the 19th century, a workweek in Belgium was approximately 70 hours – almost double the workweek today. Moreover, the work was harder, unhealthier and more dangerous than it is today. The wages were also much lower than they are today – even with a workweek that was twice as long.

The trend toward decreased working hours is clearly depicted in illustration 24. There we see the evolution of average annual working hours from the end of the 19th century to the beginning of the twentieth.

This is just one more illustration of how economic growth and wealth do not have to be synonymous with materialism. We have also used our increased wealth and affluence to collectively purchase more leisure time. That's the good thing about economic growth: the wealthier we become, the less we all have to work, thanks to the technological progress, innovation and productivity increases that make it possible.

It is thus perfectly possible for wealth to increase while, at the same time, having to work less and less to secure it. Complete or maximum employment is an economic illusion. Innovation and productivity increases have as their goal less work for the same output. Theoretically it is even possible to imagine a society in which hardly any work is necessary in order to allow people to live an acceptable level of affluence. Historically, we are used to thinking of work as an essential part of our lifestyle. In practice, this is an optical illusion. As people we are interested in greater wealth. Work is a means of creating this wealth and innovation is a way of allowing its creation to be founded on increasingly less work. There is no indication to suggest that this evolution will suddenly come to an end.

THEN WHY DO WE HAVE TO WORK LONGER?

Over the long term, working less is a sign of progress. This is proved by the experience of recent history. Growing affluence and an increase in leisure time have gone hand in hand over the last few centuries. Seen in this way, don't early retirement schemes represent a great contribution to our wealth? Why are we always being asked

Illustration 25: **Wealth by instalments**
Source: International Monetary Fund (April 2013), *World Economic Outlook*
(G7: Canada, France, Germany, Italy, Japan, United States, United Kingdom)

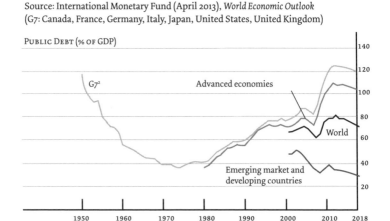

to work longer? Why does everyone say that soon we'll have to work until we're 70?

The answer is simple: less work does not in and of itself ensure more wealth, it is made possible – read: financed – by wealth. A society that becomes wealthier has a whole variety of choices about what to do with those extra means: better roads, more nature reserves, more public parking, free education, more money for fighting poverty, longer maternity leave, ski slopes in the desert, more environmental protection measures or ... not working as long.

The problem in Belgium, and by extension in the West, is that we have distributed benefits without having enough wealth to pay for them. We have, in other words, leveraged prosperity that we haven't really earned. We have made inactivity possible – unemployment, career interruption, transitional retirement, shortened careers, 35-hour workweeks, etc. – that was not immediately compensated by extra growth, wealth or income. The best proof of this is the structural increase of government deficits in the West since the 1970s.

Under normal circumstances, wealth or affluence must be created before it can be spent. The fact that government debt has climbed sharply in recent decades means that we have in fact done the opposite. In other words: we have had a glimpse of wealth that was not yet earned. These extra expenses were not financed by acquired wealth, but taken on as additional debts. This is clearly depicted in illustration 25: government debt as a percentage of total wealth (gross domestic product) has increased in recent decades. That is, the government's debts increased faster than wealth could be created.

Moreover, it was not just the government's debts that grew rapidly. Families, banks and businesses have also gone into more debt in the last few decades. Satisfying social needs by running up debts has created the feeling that society was actually making rapid progress. This was also an illusion. However you choose to see it: debts are always a claim on future wealth that has yet to be created.

It is entirely possible that, within a century, we will all study until we are 30, then work part-time for the next 20 years, and finally retire around the age of 50 and enjoy another 40 years of retirement benefits. Does that sound extreme? Working less yet still creating more wealth is exactly what we have been doing over the past 200 years.

For the time being, however, we will first have to repay the debts of the past. Over the short term we will have to work a little longer. But the long-term trend is still sound: within 50 years we will all work less than we do today.

REDISTRIBUTING WORK DOES NOT CREATE WEALTH

In times of economic crisis or recession, the argument always crops up that distributing work will help crank up the economy again or stimulate the growth of wealth. The system of early retirement was introduced precisely for this reason. If older people would stop working sooner, they would 'make room' for younger people. This assertion proceeds from the so-called *lump of labor*. If you assume that the available quantity of labor is a fixed and unchangeable lump, then someone unemployed can only find a job if someone else quits theirs.

We can be very clear about this theory: the assertion that a redistribution of labor leads to more wealth is completely absurd. Wealth does not equal employment. Wealth equals the total added value. Period. Regardless of whether that value is added by five, five million or five billion people. Distributing work among more people does absolutely nothing to increase wealth. Better yet: it destroys wealth.

No one describes this better than the important 19th-century French economist and philosopher Frédéric Bastiat in his metaphor of the negative railroad. In order to expose the conservatism of his contemporaries, he proposed – ironically – to interrupt the railroad line between Bayonne and Paris, in Bordeaux. There, passengers would be obliged to transfer to the train that would take them to Paris. Interrupting the line would create work for all the vendors, station chiefs, train personnel and hotel owners in Bordeaux. Of course, other cities would soon become jealous of the economic advantages enjoyed by Bordeaux thanks to the interruption of the railroad line. It would not be long before Angoulême, Poitiers, Tours and Orléans began demanding similar interruptions. The introduction of interruptions and inefficiency would, of course, lead to the creation of a multitude of various jobs. At the same time, it is immediately clear that these interruptions would occur at the cost of common interest. Who, at that moment – when the railroad line is full of interruptions – would still dare to argue for a direct, uninterrupted connection? One would have to fight the entire lobby of vendors, hotel owners, machinists and station chiefs who would use their power to resist the introduction of a direct train connection between Bayonne and Paris. Because eliminating the interruptions and the reintroduction of a direct line "would inevitably result in unemployment." Of course, organizing inefficiency ensures more employment for a specific number of groups. But at the same time, it also brings about a decrease in wealth for everyone. The redistribution of labor at the expense of wealth is pure madness.

From this perspective it would, for example, be entirely possible to have everyone fully employed in Belgium. Prohibit the use of bulldozers and trench diggers starting next year, and oblige everyone to use shovels. Employment would increase dramatically: to do the same work in building construction, laying roads, mining or even gardening, would require many times the employees needed today. If anyone were still unemployed after that, the remedy would be just as simple: forbid the use of spades and require the use of spoons instead. Many hundreds of thousands of extra people would then have a job. Hurray! Everyone would be 'employed', but wealth as such would decline as a result.

There are an endless number of ways to drive up employment artificially. Prohibiting traffic lights will ensure a spectacular increase in employment among traffic police. At the same time, traffic will flow less smoothly and wealth will decrease. Forbidding parking sensors will create more work for auto repair shops. At the same time, people will lose more time thanks to minor collisions, filling in claims and visiting the mechanic, and thus wealth will also decrease. Halving the tonnage allowance of freight trucks will double the number of trucks needed and thereby create more jobs in the transport sector. At the same time, it will lead to more traffic, more traffic jams and more costly transportation costs, and thus wealth will decrease. Prohibiting automatic sliding doors will create thousands of jobs for porters. At the same time, managing and maintaining buildings will become more expensive, and wealth reduced. Forbidding tractors and threshing machines will ensure a spectacular increase in employment in the agricultural sector. At the same time, it will make agricultural products more expensive, thereby reducing wealth. Retiring older workers at the age of 55 will apparently create jobs for the young. In practice, it only makes all labor more expensive – because the larger number of people who are made inactive will have to be supported with tax money. By making all labor more expensive – including that of young people – employment opportunities are eliminated and wealth decreases.

The number of jobs created is hardly a measure of increasing wealth. The total value added is.

JOB DESTRUCTION AND LEISURE AS SIGNS OF WEALTH

Wealth is created by the addition of value: by inventing, by competing, by innovating, by creating new products, by introducing better production processes... The past two centuries have provided the best proof of this. They have witnessed one innovation and improvement after the other, all of which have made us collectively wealthier, healthier, older and happier. The jobs we do take up less of our time and affect our health less than ever before. An average Belgian today enjoys a level of health, life expectancy and standard of living that even kings and noblemen in the middle ages could only dream of.

The future doom scenario in which we will be collectively obliged to work until we are 100 is totally unfounded. It is more likely that the opposite will be the case. Scientific research and innovations will make people more productive and enable them to work less and less hard, while at the same time, adding more value. The West no longer employs half of its population in agriculture. This is thanks to the tractor, fertilizers, better seeds, genetic modification and better farming techniques. We have devoted an inordinate amount of the collective increase in our life expectancy and affluence to extra leisure time over the past two centuries. That we now have to work longer today is just a temporary phenomenon. After all, we have taken an advance on wealth that we have not yet created. As for the future, more wealth, less work and more free time are the most realistic estimate.

A capitalist system is constantly in motion. Through competition, innovation and changing consumer preferences. New sectors and jobs appear and cause other industries or jobs to disappear. Unfortunately, the focus today is all too often on the short-term: the uncertainty and the unrest generated by closing companies, sharp competition and the decline of jobs and sectors. What is lost is visible. What will take its place is not yet visible. We need, then, to learn to look past the madness of the day and spot the long-term opportunities. The process of creative destruction is often presented as a *negative sum game*: with society and citizens as the losers against the free market and merciless competition. Not so. The one-sided focus on shutdowns and job loss – in the steel or automobile sectors, for example – makes us completely blind to new opportunities in biotechnology, IT, new forms of energy and 3-D printing. In reality, creative destruction is a *positive sum game*: society as a whole progresses thanks to new opportunities, new products, new services and a higher standard of living.

The best answer to all those who are pessimistic about the free market and innovation can be summed up in one word: 'agriculture'. No other sector has seen more job destruction in the past century than agriculture. In the West, many tens of millions of jobs were lost. At the same time, food today is more available, more accessible, safer, more nourishing *and* cheaper than a hundred years ago. Of course, all those innovations and improvements to productivity decimated agricultural employment, but they also ensured giant steps forward for society as a whole in terms of wealth.

And so we come back to the beginning: job destruction and job creation are the yin and yang of wealth. One does not exist without the other. As long as we continue to innovate and compete, we will continue to create wealth. And as long as we create wealth, we will become richer, healthier, grow older and have to work less and less. On the condition that we keep creating wealth...

PRODUCTIVITY, WEALTH AND LEISURE TIME

What is the connection between productivity, wealth and leisure time? In the preceding chapters, we have already seen that the increase in productivity made it possible to work less while still achieving the same amount of wealth. The evidence of recent centuries proves that we have gone even further in practice: we work even less, yet at the same time, we have greatly increased our total wealth.

A concrete example can be useful for isolating the different mechanisms. Let's take a country with two corn farmers: Tom and Dick. They each have a field of ten hectares on which they grow corn. Each works his field with the same primitive techniques. They both work 60 hours per week and during harvest season they both achieve an identical yield of one ton of corn per hectare. The total corn production of the country in question is thus equal to 20 tons. Depending on the demand for corn, the farmers get a price of 100 ducats per ton. For each harvest, Tom and Dick both earn 1,000 ducats each. The following year, Tom decides to use his savings to buy a tractor and other mechanized farming equipment. This saves him a great deal of labor: from then on he succeeds in working his entire ten hectares of land in half the time it takes his neighbor Dick. The total harvest and

Illustration 26: **Wealth and productivity**

		Tom	Dick	Total	
1	Corn (tons)	10	10	20	Initial conditions
2	Work (hours per week)	60	60	120	
1/2	Productivity	0.17	0.17	0.17	
1	Corn (tons)	10	10	20	Tom buys a tractor and works less
2	Work (hours per week)	30	60	90	
1/2	Productivity	0.33	0.17	0.22	
1	Corn (tons)	20	10	30	Tom has a tractor but decides to work more
2	Work (hours per week)	60	60	120	
1/2	Productivity	0.33	0.17	0.25	

143

the price per ton remains the same. The only difference is that Tom has only had to work half the time to achieve the same result. Whatever the price of corn turns out to be, Tom's income per hour worked will be double that of Dick's. His investment in higher productivity has been completely converted into less work, but not greater production volume. By halving his working hours, Tom has increased his personal wealth. He can take more time off, read a book or spend more time with his family.

A year later Tom decides to start working 60 hours per week again. By working 60-hour weeks – this time with a tractor and mechanized farm equipment – he succeeds in driving up his yield to two tons per hectare. His harvest will be double that of Dick's. When both farmers bring their corn harvest to market, there is an additional 30 tons of corn available. Because the corn supply has increased by 50% but the demand has remained the same, the price drops to 80 ducats per ton. If Tom supplied a total of 20 tons, he has a profit of 1,600 ducats. Dick still supplies ten tons, but at a market price of 80 ducats, his income drops to 800 ducats. Again it is clear – this time financially – that Tom has produced an added value that is twice as high as before. His investments in machinery and tractors have clearly delivered results. On the whole, the farmers earn more than before the introduction of new technology: they earn 2,400 ducats as opposed to 2,000. Between the farmers themselves, however, something has changed: inequality has increased. Tom earns twice as much as Dick. Growth has resulted in more inequality (see also chapter 6). Illustration 26 shows schematically the different scenarios for Tom, Dick and society at large.

Finally, society as a whole has also benefited. The population has a greater available supply of corn (30 tons instead of 20), and at a lower price (8 ducats instead of 10). The improvements to productivity may have resulted in greater inequality among the farmers themselves, but both society as a whole and the farmers as a group have made progress.

As to what happens next, there are various possible scenarios. There is a very good chance that Tom – thanks to his greater productivity and income – will continue to invest in further increasing his productivity. In this way, he will drive up the total supply of corn even more. Society as a whole will be very content with this trend: because the consumer is confronted with a greater supply at even lower prices, the standard of living has been raised once again. Thanks to Investments in more productive agriculture, they pay less for corn and have more money left over for other things. If Tom continues to invest in productivity, Dick, by contrast, will have a difficult time of it and will earn even less from his harvest. He can still try to work more than 60 hours per week, but even that is not really a solution. He will not be able to compete with the greater, mechanized productivity of his neighbor Tom. In that case the conclusion is clear: Tom's investments are advantageous to himself and to the population at large. Those who stay behind and do not invest in higher productivity will be increasingly marginalized.

Another possibility is that Dick too begins to invest in an improvement of his productivity. A cooperation agreement between the two farmers and increase in scale is another possibility that can prove advantageous for all parties involved. Finally, Dick could also offer to sell or rent (some of) his land to Tom. In this way, he could open a corn restaurant or a popcorn factory. Thanks to Tom's innovations, the population has to spend a smaller portion of its income on staple foods. Consequently, they have to work less to make ends meet and have more leisure time and disposable income for eating out in restaurants or buying popcorn. This is also an important finding: the only reason why 'Dick the restaurateur' or 'Dick the popcorn mogul' can be successful is because 'Dick the farmer' had to face stiff competition from his neighbor Tom.

Ultimately, everybody has moved ahead. Before he purchased tractors and mechanized farming equipment, Tom had to work long and hard and managed to earn very little from his efforts. Today, Tom is more productive and richer than ever.

Dick had a difficult time at first. Because his neighbor innovated and he did not, he earned less and less money for his labor and ran into financial problems. For this reason he decided to consider another career. Now he is the owner of a large popcorn factory and a restaurant. He earns much more today than he did as a farmer.

The population as a whole has also made considerable progress. Thanks to innovation and competition, they have a wider assortment of products from which to choose. Moreover, they don't have to spend as much on food as they did in the past. The result is that they now have more time and more money to spend on all kinds of other goods and services, such as a meal in a restaurant or popcorn.

The moral of the story: it is the uninterrupted stream of competition and innovation between Tom and Dick that ultimately benefits Tom, Dick ... and Harry.

CHAPTER 9

Obstacles on the road to growth

"Demography is destiny." — **Auguste Comte**,
French philosopher of science (1798-1857) and inventor
of the term 'sociology'

*"With some notable exceptions, businessmen favor free
enterprise in general but are opposed to it when it comes to
themselves."* — **Milton Friedman**

*"You cannot protect something by building a fence
around it and hoping this will help it survive."*
— **Wim Wenders**, German film director
and documentary maker (°1945)

*"Powerful groups often stand against economic progress
and against the engines of prosperity. Economic growth is
not just a process of more and better machines, and more
and better educated people, but also a transformative and
destabilizing process associated with widespread creative
destruction. Growth thus moves forward only if not blocked
by the economic losers who anticipate that their economic
privileges will be lost and by the political losers who fear
that their political power will be eroded."*
— **Daron Acemoglu and James A. Robinson**,
economists and authors of the book *Why Nations Fail*

To those for whom it is not yet clear: growth is embedded in our human DNA. It touches on the deep desire and ineradicable ambition to improve one's own situation in every possible way. Only when people have the complete freedom to become entrepreneurs, to invest, to compete and to innovate, is wealth actually created. In theory, at any rate. In practice, there are many, many obstacles on the road to creating wealth. From too few young people to too many debts. From companies that don't have any competitors to companies that don't want any competitors. From clinging to the status quo to avoiding risk.

Some obstacles are inevitable, or at least extremely difficult to avoid: demography is one of them. The aging of the European population can be compared with a large glacier: immense, slow moving, with a predictable path over the next few years and destructive to whatever lies in that path. Other obstacles can be more or less cleared away: an addiction to debt, the reign of interest groups, an aversion to risk or a predilection for the status quo.

DEMOGRAPHY: OLDER, MORE EXPENSIVE, SLOWER

The most noticeable restraint on the growth of wealth in the years and decades to come is the evolution of Western demography. In chapter 7, we saw how the majority of the Western world has already gone through the entire spectrum of demographic transition. At the very beginning of that transition – a high birth rate and decreasing death rate – the number of young people in the population increases spectacularly. At the very end – a stagnating population and a dramatically increased life expectancy – the number of old people increases dramatically. This development has a double effect. In the first place it ensures a spectacular increase in the costs of growing older: retirement benefits, healthcare and relief measures. At the same time, the earning capacity of the economy is put under pressure by the decreasing number of (qualified) young people needed to replace the large group of old people leaving the job market. In many

European countries the working-age population – people between the ages of 15 and 65 who are able to work – will reach its peak in the years to come and then begin to decline.

Over the long term, the total growth of wealth is determined by the growth of the population on the one hand and the growth of productivity on the other. Put another way: the growth of the number of people who can add value and the degree to which they can add value. The first has to do with individual choices that are made in the bedroom; the second is the result of both individual and collective choices relating to education, innovation, research and development, entrepreneurship and willingness to take risks. From illustration 27 it is evident that the factor population growth will turn against the growth of wealth in Europe in the years to come. The graph shows the moment at which the active, working population in each country reaches its peak. The larger the circle, the larger the active population when the population peaks. From the peak onward, there are fewer people available to work. In practice, they can even have a negative effect, and usually do. The only way to allow wealth to grow from that moment on is to increase productivity and create a better climate for entrepreneurship.

What also stands out is that today, countries like Japan or Germany have already passed their demographic peaks. It is no wonder that robots that can play soccer, make a bed or serve food nearly always seem to come from Japan. This is the only kind of productivity improvements that can offer a counterweight to the declining number of people on the job market. The labor population of Germany will also shrink in the next 20 years by more than five million people. Although the German economy today is still hovering near its zenith, the demographic shrinkage of the coming decades threatens to become a time bomb ticking away under the economic success story. Within Europe, France seems to be in the best shape demographically. As is the United States, it may be added. In both countries, labor potential will reach its peak after 2100.

The global success story – in terms of demography – is Africa: there, demography is anything but an obstacle. The United Nations expects the African population to triple in the 21st century: from approximately one billion today to more than 3.5 billion by the end of the century. The majority of the large African countries will see their labor population stabilize after 2100. In combination with catching up on agriculture, productivity, political transparency, education and technology, there is immense growth potential for this continent. But this does require that we stop seeing Africans as permanently needy victims, and instead view them as an immense group of people on the eve of a great leap forward. A leap forward that is largely held back by bad institutions, old technology, corruption and a lack of free markets and freedom.

"Demography is destiny," said French sociologist Auguste Comte in the 19th century. Death rates and birth rates, in his view, determined the entire future of countries and continents. This is perhaps

Illustration 27: **Demographic deficit in Europe**
Source: Boston Consulting Group (January 2013), *Ending the Era of Ponzi Finance*

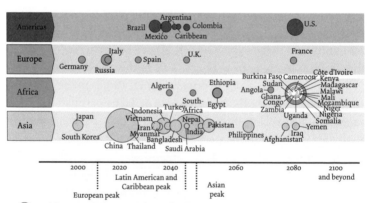

Workforce population at peak (100 million)
Sources: United Nations, *World population prospects*, 2010 revision, June 2011; BCG Analysis.
Note: The labor force consists of all people ages 15 to 64. This exhibit shows only countries with a peak labor force of 30 million or more; data includes the impact of immigration.

an overstatement: we still have our destiny in our own hands. Nevertheless, demography is particularly important: it determines the boundaries of what is financially and economically possible. The negative European demography of the coming decades means that we will have to make every possible effort where other sources of growth are concerned: competition, innovation, a positive climate for entrepreneurship, research and development and education.

DEBT: WEALTH BY INSTALLMENTS

Once there was a successful entrepreneur. He led a fast-growing company with a large turnover and splendid annual profits. With that money, he could eat at a fancy restaurant a couple of times a week, take his family on exotic vacations every three months and every two years or so park a new sports car in the driveway. Gradually – and without it really being noticeable at first – the company's turnover began to peter out and its profits grew smaller year after year. The entrepreneur didn't want to tell his wife and children that things weren't going quite so well with the business. Then he would have to tell them that there would be fewer restaurant meals, the vacations would be less exotic and that the sports car would have to stand in the driveway a little longer. Then he discovered the existence of credit: he began to borrow more and more money in order to maintain his lifestyle. His promise of future growth in turnover and profit served as collateral for the loans. No one seemed to notice that there was a problem: they dined just as often in restaurants, exotic vacations were still possible and there was still a new sports car in the driveway every two years. There didn't really seem to be any need to restructure the company, look for new sources of income or adjust his and his family's lifestyle. In the meantime the debts piled up higher and higher. The loans also had a double effect: in the first place they ensured a constantly increasing pile of debt, while at the same time, they blinded the entrepreneur to the reality of his failing enterprise. The increasingly greater difference between crumbling growth potential and mounting debts was already problematic in itself. Against the background of an unchanged lifestyle and the illusion of wealth, the catastrophe was complete.

The example above is a brief summary of Western economic growth and debt position in recent decades. An increasingly large debt structure, the illusion of continually growing wealth and the crumbling of underlying growth potential. Debts encourage procrastination. Because, let's be honest: the sports car, the exotic vacations and the restaurant dinners constitute 'the illusion of wealth' when they have to be paid for with credit. In themselves, debts do not have to be negative. Debts that are made to finance productive investments, for example, are not necessarily a problem. The investment itself heightens growth potential and guarantees the repayment of the debts. For this reason, it is perfectly acceptable to finance a new highway network, new computers, a better education system or a new piece of equipment with debt. However, when debts are made to finance current consumption levels, there is definitely a problem. That much is clear from the example above: if the entrepreneur had made debts in order to reinvest in his business, there would have been nothing wrong. But when the debts are made in order to pay for an increasingly opulent lifestyle, without looking at the underlying earning potential, there is definitely something wrong. Of course, this is the problem of many Western countries. The largest piece of the debt structure in recent decades was used to finance transfers, the redistribution of wealth and additional welfare – not for productive investments. In Belgium we have hired scores of bureaucrats but have neglected the state of our roads; we have greatly expanded social welfare programs but have barely succeeded in computerizing government administration; we guarantee everyone wages that are indexed to offset inflation, but don't succeed in educating the children of immigrants sufficiently enough to make them fellow citizens of standing...

In practice, the West has purchased wealth wholesale on the installment plan in recent decades. This debt structure has made possible economic growth, the additional expansion of government and social services. This has made the West blind to the structural decline of the underlying growth potential. The following generation will thus have to pay off the debts of the past before it can once again think about further expansion of the welfare state.

THE EUROZONE: THE PRICE OF OVERCONFIDENCE

The current debacle surrounding the Eurozone is a variation on the theme of the illusion of wealth. On the surface, sharing a currency among 17 countries seemed to embody the idea of a genuine monetary union. Our present reality shows that a lot more is needed to make this monetary union work properly. A real political union is the prerequisite for a smoothly functioning monetary union. But that construction was not possible 15 years ago. So in effect, we decided to erect a building with the same façade, ignoring the fact that the foundations were acquired at a hefty discount. Today, the building is beginning to collapse and expensive reinforcements have to be introduced. It is the Great Building of the European Federation that is costing us money, wealth and political capital. That is the price we must pay for a Euro-project that was set up in overconfidence and haste.

European leaders in the 1990s used the fall of the Iron Curtain as a flywheel for the additional, far-reaching integration of Europe. Because setting up a real European Republic was a bridge too far, it was decided that a common currency would be introduced. Some countries – Germany in particular – did not agree with this approach. The Germans were advocates of the so-called 'theory of the coronation', in which a common currency would crown the successful political unification of Europe. This is the way things had happened in the history of Germany itself. But in the discussion surrounding the organization of Europe at the time, Germany unfortunately got the short end of the stick. For the other European leaders, a political union would take far too long; the introduction of a common currency was a faster way to realize a quick win.

Now politicians find to their dismay that they have indeed installed a Euro-crown, but that the political and economic foundations are built on shifting sand. Thanks to the euro, every individual country is indeed dependent on the remaining 16. A real estate bubble in Spain, lax bank supervision in Ireland, wage politics in Germany, the length of the workweek in France, the extension of credit in Italy, wage indexing in Belgium, corruption and budgetary policy in Greece… Each of these supposedly domestic themes has consequences for Europe as a whole. Yet while financial panic, liquidity trends, weak growth and crumbling confidence cross borders without problems and at lightning speed, the strategies for combating crises remains domestic to a significant degree.

A European Federation with fixed rules and agreements would certainly be a clear improvement over the present approach. But we should have thought of that when the monetary union was still in the making. Organizing bank supervision, emergency funds, deposit protection, bailout plans, supervising modernization and reform and drawing up budgetary measures not only cost time and money, they also result in painful uncertainty. Organizing a political and economic union while the whole process is already underway inevitably takes place at the expense of economic growth in Europe.

The fact that we still have to cobble together an entire economic, structural, financial and political foundation – in real time – under the Euro-crown costs us not only wealth, but also a great deal of political capital. Just as each euro can only be spent once, political capital can only be used once. Modernizing the economy costs politicians popularity. Reducing government debt – through higher taxes or lower government expenditures – has the same effect. A recession also makes politicians vulnerable. If on top of that you combine these three problems with the permanent transfer of authority from sovereign member states to 'Brussels', you are flirting with the limits of what the population and voters find acceptable today. This limits the rate at which we can make progress with the Great Federation Building and spreads the economic pain over an extended period.

To be perfectly clear: there is no way back. Whether we like it or not: the countries now in the monetary union are monetarily, economically and financially anchored to one another. Tearing this anchorage apart would come at a gigantic cost: economically, financially and politically. The only way back would be a return to the old national currencies which would prove even more expensive than what we experience today. Our present problems cannot be solved with the tools we ordinarily have in our macro-economic toolbox. The conclusion is as simple as it is painful: there is no magic formula for conjuring up economic growth. Modernizing and cleaning up economies is painful enough as it is. That we have to build a European Federation on top of it is costing us considerable wealth today. With the euro, visionary politicians introduced us to the greatest level of European integration in history. These same politicians, however, sowed the seeds of the present malaise with their overconfidence.

MONOPOLIES AND PROTECTIONISM: NO COMPETITION PLEASE!

Monopolists are companies that don't have any competitors. Protectionists are companies that don't want any competitors. Both monopolies and protectionism cost a society in terms of wealth: in the form of higher prices, less freedom of choice and poorer quality products and services. In both cases, society as a whole sacrifices wealth in order to finance the privileges of a small group.

Monopolists are companies that are the only ones offering a particular product. Thus, there are no competitors to keep them on their toes. Since citizens can only turn to the monopolists in question for these products – rail transportation, air travel, telephone service or energy needs – they have no interest in lowering their prices, innovating or improving the quality of their products or services. Those who are unsatisfied have nowhere else to go. That makes life a great deal easier for the monopolist, but it is bad news for all citizens and consumers. Those who impede competition, limit innovation.

155

Those who limit innovation, destroy wealth. The classic example is that of the earlier state monopolies on telephone service. Requesting and installing a telephone line could take weeks, service was particularly bad and the price was far too high. Those who want to use the telephone today can buy a telephone with prepaid calling time at the supermarket in less than five minutes.

Monopolies have existed for a long time. Throughout history, monopolies on certain goods or services were often granted by princes, dictators or the ruling political class. In exchange for generous payments or services rendered, the sector received a monopoly. The best-known example in history is that of the medieval guilds: the guild of the weavers, the carpenters, the butchers, the brewers, the blacksmiths... They were the prototype groups that protected their own interests and, in this way, held the wealth of the entire population in check. Those who are protected against competition become lazy, stop innovating and offer consumers substandard products at exaggerated prices. Monopolies are thus also a major obstacle to economic growth and progress. Monopolists hate the free market and deny society the chance to move forward.

Protectionism is likewise a mockery of the free market and a check on wealth. Here we are concerned with companies that do everything possible to make it difficult for foreign competitors to gain access to their own domestic market (see the box "Guide to effective protectionism"). This can be accomplished by the erection of trade barriers, import prohibition, import duties, export subsidies, environmental norms, social norms and the like. In practice, it might be an import duty on Chinese tires, an import prohibition against Chinese solar panels, an import duty on African vegetables or American beef... In reality this is a form of disguised support for particular national sectors at the expense of the consumer.

There are two negative consequences associated with this policy. In the first place, consumers are denied access to cheaper products and better services. Protectionism obliges them to choose domestic producers, even when they sell inferior products at higher prices. A second effect of protectionism is retaliation. After all, there's a good chance that the other party (the country affected by protectionism) will decide to respond with its own protectionist measures. This could come in the form of levying import duties or closing the borders to particular products. The sectors affected by retaliatory protectionism are the dupes.

In the case of both protectionism and monopolies, the interests of a small group of producers take precedence over the interests of society as a whole. The latter are forced to sacrifice wealth. Whether we are faced with an import duty on foreign agricultural products, export subsidies for European agricultural products or an import duty on Chinese solar panels, the consumer is the dupe every time. He or she is forced to buy more expensive products solely because a limited lobby group has succeeded in wresting special treatment from politicians.

Protectionism makes companies temporary monopolists in practice: poorer quality and higher prices for the consumer *and* a lack of innovation. Moreover, it weakens the sector itself in the long run. Ex-monopolists often have a hard time surviving in a competitive market. Companies that have been able to take refuge temporarily in the hothouse of protectionism often suffer the slings and arrows of outrageous fortune when they come back out again. Naturally because they're no longer used to competing and innovating.

The conclusion is clear and concise: monopolists and protectionists cost society wealth. Society as a whole pays the price for the temporary protection of the few – a protection that works counterproductively. Monopolies and protectionism destroy wealth – both short- and long-term.

There are many different ways for countries to shut out competition with foreign producers. The most effective of these is just to close the borders to particular foreign products. Because this form of protectionism is fairly obvious, the country disadvantaged by it can dispute it before authorities such as the World Trade Organization (WTO). Moreover, there is the risk that the affected trade partner will retaliate by closing its own borders to the products of the original protectionist. In this way, a policy of open protectionism threatens to fly back in one's face like a boomerang.

Another way to make things more difficult for foreign competitors is to subject imported products to an import duty. In this way, foreign products are made artificially expensive for domestic consumers and domestic producers have a slight advantage in selling their products. The greater the original price difference in comparison to domestic producers, the greater the duty usually is. Or in other words: the greater the competition from abroad, the greater the duty. The duty serves a highly specific goal: to cancel out the competitive advantage of the imported products, or even transform it into a disadvantage.

The import of Japanese cars into Europe, for example, is subject to duties of around 10%. From the moment the cars in question drive off the ship and into the showroom, they are thus 10% more expensive for European consumers. France is the most avid proponent of this policy. Many Japanese cars compete directly in the segment that also includes French brands such as Renault, Peugeot and Citroën. The import duties are a way of making things easier for French producers. Of course, it is the European consumer who pays for the protection of the European auto sector. Try the following test: deduct 10% from the book price of a Japanese car and find out how much cheaper it would be without protectionism. Or try the reverse: what is the price that every Toyota or Mazda driver pays today in order to protect the interests – read: inefficiency – of the European auto industry?

Many imported agricultural products are subject to all manner of duties in order to protect the European agricultural sector. The import of American beef, for example, is subject to duties of 100%. That is to say that the price of a 500 gram steak doubles just by crossing the Atlantic Ocean. If a duty of 100% is needed to eliminate the competitive advantage of American meat, it is immediately clear how many Europeans are paying too much for their meat these days.

Another subtle form of protectionism is the awarding of state support or subsidies to particular domestic sectors. This allows domestic producers to decrease the price of their own products so that they are immediately competitive with imports from abroad. It is an open secret, for example, that the American aircraft manufacturer Boeing receives indirect subsidies from the government in the form of enormously costly, non-competitive defense contracts. For the production and maintenance of American military planes, contracts are often concluded with Boeing. Because it concerns defense, the argument of national security is often invoked to reject the bids of foreign competitors. Because Boeing receives a quasi-monopoly on defense contracts in this way, it can demand unreasonably high prices in practice. With the money that the firm has left over from those far too generous defense contracts, it can keep the cost of its civilian aircraft artificially low. And there you have it, mission accomplished: when international airline companies compare incoming bids for new airplanes, Airbus – Boeing's European competitor – is not automatically the best in terms of price-quality ratio. Or how government money from defense contracts is partly intended as a way of making things difficult for foreign manufacturers of civilian aircraft.

European agriculture policy likewise awards generous subsidies to European farmers. Although the greatest distortions caused by this policy have since been adjusted in the meantime, the subsidies nevertheless make things more difficult for foreign competitors. Because European farmers receive subsidies, it is more difficult for foreign farmers to bring their products to market. A budget of around 60 billion euros per year is dedicated to protecting the European agricultural market. The perverse aspect of this situation is that the European taxpayer pays twice. She has in the first place to pay taxes, which are then used to keep the price of her vegetables, fruit, meat and restaurant visits artificially expensive.

Another – and much subtler – way of resisting foreign products is the introduction of technical standards or tests. Although technical norms in and of themselves are not usually meant as a form of protectionism, this is frequently a welcome side effect nonetheless. By imposing certain technical norms, it becomes more difficult for foreign producers to gain access to the market. In Japan, for example, there is a category of small city car known as the *Kei Car*. This type of car enjoys a highly favorable tax regime: a reduced registration tax and a very low category of road tax. The volume of both the car and the engine is very small. The current version has an engine volume of only 660 cc. This category of car is roughly equivalent to that of the Austin Mini or Fiat 500, for example, both of which should find a ready market in Japan for this reason. The Japanese government, however, insists on a maximum engine volume of 660 cc and for now refuses to allow European cars into the Japanese market. For European auto manufacturers, developing a new and smaller engine exclusively for the Japanese market would be a cost they could scarcely earn back – and so the Japanese market for small cars effectively remains closed to European producers. Moreover, assemblers from other countries are not easily admitted into the Japanese market. The net result is that today, there is only one type of Kei Car that is not made in Japan: the Smart K. This alone proves that technical standards are a handy and perfidious means of eliminating foreign competition altogether.

Another example: Audi, Mercedes and Toyota have recently developed a new sort of headlight that enables driving at night with the high beams continually running. The car's electronic sensors register the approach of oncoming traffic and dim part of the lights automatically. In this way, approaching drivers are not blinded and the rest of the road is well lit. This combination would, of course, enhance the safety of all drivers. American law is such, however, that this innovation is not permitted there. That means European and Japanese auto manufacturers would have to spend more on development only to be admitted into the United States. The separate rules force auto manufacturers to make expensive adjustments to their models. If they don't – and thus install the headlights of the previous generation – they deny the consumer the possibility of choosing a better and safer car.

Tests and standards are also frequently used to protect domestic markets in the pharmaceutical industry. A medicine developed in the United States must still undergo an entire – and often identical – battery of tests in order to be accepted on grounds of public health, effectiveness, toxicity and the like. Of course, the same thing happens when a European producer wants to launch a new medicine on the American market. Insisting on carrying out the entire battery of screenings and tests once again gives domestic producers on both sides a *de facto* advantage. Although a unified process of approval for new medicines would be much cheaper and more efficient for both consumers and government finances, in practice it would go directly against the interests of local pharmaceutical companies. They would suddenly have to take foreign competition much more seriously. The tests and acceptance procedures did not come into being as a conscious barrier against foreign competitors. In practice, though, they have that effect.

As we have just seen, there are no limits to the inventiveness and creativity of countries when it comes to making things difficult for foreign competitors and protecting domestic producers. The biggest victim is always the consumer, who is forced to pay high prices for a more limited choice of products. Just imagine how much better the world would be for consumers and citizens if countries invested their energy, creativity and inventiveness in developing better and newer products, services and innovations instead of stingily trying to keep those same products, services, or innovations out of their own markets. Just because they come from abroad.

The American economist Mancur Olson describes in his classic 1982 book *The Rise and Decline of Nations* how special interest groups all too often succeed in hijacking the common good and, in this way, cripple the growth of wealth. Interest groups are characterized by the fact that they represent their own members, but not society as a whole. In their dealings with the government on taxes, subsidies or exemption regimes, they will always represent their own group's interests first and not those of society as a whole.

Interest groups often weigh disproportionately on policy. The reason is simple: a lobby of wine producers, doctors, farmers, shopkeepers or pharmacists is easier to unite around a specific theme than society as a whole, which is highly diverse and heterogeneous. For this reason alone, interest groups or lobbies are better organized on average and will be able to make their demands and interests much more visible than those of society as a whole. As a result, they will also succeed more easily in having their specific demands accepted, even if they go against the interests of society.

The calculus of interest groups can be expressed with a simple formula:

$$\text{individual interest x size of organization} = \text{media attention} = \text{political attention}$$

A well-organized group in which every member stands to win/lose a great deal with every specific measure taken/proposed will receive more attention from the media and from politicians. That's what interest groups are. Examples abound: farmers, lawyers, banks, industrial concerns, train mechanics or telecommunications companies. Each of these interest groups has a great deal to win/lose from changes in policy enacted by the government and will therefore not fail to bring these to the attention of the media and politicians. A poorly organized group in which the members do not stand to win/lose very much from the same measures will receive much less attention from the media and politicians. One good example: the taxpayer, the citizen. The results are clear: every interest group succeeds relatively easily in prizing loose advantages; the unorganized taxpayer or citizen will have to pay for their success.

The result is thus a proliferation of specific subsidies, advantageous measures, financial concessions, sales tax reductions, exceptional statuses and protection against competition. They are made to measure for specific sectors, such as solar panels, wind turbines, restaurants, bars and hotels or farmers – but they damage society as a whole.

The kinds of concessions we are talking about do not have the common good in mind. Subsidies and tax deductions, for example, are not 'free'. They are paid for with tax money (see also the box "Subsidies create losers").

Subsidies are, moreover, fairly expensive. Every subsidy demands a separate application form, an administration to follow up the applications, a commission to pass judgment and finally another administration that follows up and monitors all the allocations. It would probably just be more efficient to replace the most specific subsidies with a subsidy for every individual citizen and every individual business. It would not only reduce the tax burden, but from then on citizens and businesses could decide for themselves what to spend money on, without being 'directed' by subsidies or tax rebates. Rather than letting the government tell them what to spend money on, people can do a better job of it themselves. Unfortunately this sort of subsidy vanished into the mists of economic history quite some time ago. It was known as a 'tax reduction'.

All of this makes it especially difficult to do away with advantages for interest groups. A tax reduction or an increase in wealth for the entire society at the level of each individual citizen would amount to a very limited amount of progress. Insufficient progress, in fact, to get people to turn out in great numbers in support of it, are certainly not strong enough to unite a highly divergent group of citizens under a single banner. The members of interest groups have much more to lose as individuals. They will defend the preservation of their exception regimes and tax advantages tooth and nail. Because they are better organized and have more to lose, they also have megaphones and media close at hand for expressing their discontent. A small group for which much more is at stake individually is more readily heard than a large group whose members will only make a small step forward individually. And in this way, the status quo is maintained. Small groups get large advantages at the cost of wealth for society at large. Interest groups perpetuate the status quo and destroy wealth.

NO WEALTH WITHOUT RISK

The creation of wealth is never risk-free. Entrepreneurship, competition, innovation – all of these are dangerous. An entrepreneur can go bankrupt. A company or even an entire sector can be overwhelmed by the competition. Investing in the development of a new product can cost a lot of money if no one wants to buy it. Yet taking risks is still the only way to create wealth. An aversion to risk inhibits progress and the growth of wealth. Engaging in totally risk-free activities never helped a society to build up its wealth.

Frightened of what the future will bring, Belgians today are parking record amounts in their savings accounts. The lower interest rates go, the more money the anxious saver deposits. The media in turn serve us daily helpings of risk: eating untreated vegetables, walking in the sun, breathing near large highways, working too much, working too little... The interpretation of the terms 'risky' and 'risk-free' is constantly changing. Like a deer caught in the headlights of an oncoming car, we seem to see nothing but risks everywhere we look: from global warming to global terrorism, from a Japanese scenario for Europe to a Greek scenario for Belgium, from exploding populations to exploding nuclear reactors.

We find ourselves today in a climate in which everyone sees risks everywhere, and overestimates their probability and the possible consequences. This subjective evaluation of risks – their chances of occurring as well as their impact – does not make things any easier for governments. They are confronted with a population that would prefer to eliminate risk from the world entirely. All risks should be forbidden: for cyclists, patients, consumers, investors, athletes, old people, animals, banks, employees, drivers and train passengers. It's all one big battle for a single, unattainable goal: zero risks. Period.

Agreed, the experience of the financial crisis has taught us that taking too many risks can also go completely wrong. Taking political risks, such as the launch of the monetary union, has also caused damage of its own. Nevertheless: without taking risks, we destroy wealth. Not only is it an illusion to think that a risk-free world could actually exist, it is also downright dangerous. Risk is part of our human and social DNA: if our ancestors were just as averse to risk as we have become today, we would probably not be here to talk about it. Then they would never have come out of their caves to hunt for food, defend their territory or make the transition to a sedentary lifestyle. Political revolutions, medical breakthroughs, athletic feats, military operations or business successes: without taking risks, they would all be impossible. Galileo took a big risk in claiming that the earth revolved around the sun and not vice versa. Chuck Yeager knew he was taking risks when he became the first human being to break the sound barrier. Ryanair took a great risk by challenging the former air traffic monopolists. Henry Ford certainly liked risk: he had already gone bankrupt five times by the time he made his breakthrough with the mass production of personal automobiles. Without Columbus's risky decision to seek a western passage to India, we would have never had the United States. Without people who dare to take risks, progress cannot exist.

Entrepreneurs and businesses in the here and now also create wealth day in, day out by constantly taking risks. Giving a client the chance to pay later. Developing a new product. Hiring a new employee. Looking for new markets abroad. Taking over another business. These are all risks that can create wealth. As a society, we have forgotten the art of taking risks, but we expect freelancers, entrepreneurs, company executives, young start-ups and researchers to do so on our behalf. Our social security, police departments, healthcare, culture, roads and education are all paid for by people that have made taking risks their business. Those who risk nothing, risk everything. A collective longing for a risk-free welfare state is today costing us our welfare.

DIRIGISME: THE GOVERNMENT KNOWS BETTER

Certainly in times of economic crisis or economic standstill, it is always tempting for the government to try and stimulate economic growth or even to direct it. The defenders of government stimulation believe that the government must act in the place of citizens and spend money to get the economy going again. However, the defenders of government intervention forget one important question: why is the government better placed than the citizen to choose the activities on which money must be spent? Should more be spent on solar panels or geothermal energy? More research and development or more bureaucrats? More social services or more highways? More subsidies for biological cultivation or longer maternity leave?

Why should the government be better placed to make all these choices? The market is the most efficient way of translating all the preferences and desires of all those different citizens into production decisions. It is not possible for the government to group all the knowledge, desires, ambitions and plans of all citizens and companies in order to make its decisions on this basis. The disastrous experience of the planned economy of many a socialist regime has demonstrated this sufficiently. By trying to take the place of individual citizens, the government destroys wealth instead of creating it. In the first place, decisions will be made on the basis of incomplete knowledge. Moreover, the process will be less efficient than if everybody made his or her own choices. We may not forget that the government is not that good at choosing 'future winners'. In the 1960s, the French and British governments thought that supersonic air travel was the technology of the future. The inherently loss-making Concorde proved them wrong. In recent years, the governments of Belgium, Europe and the United States have pumped billions into the green energy sector: solar panels, wind turbines, alternative energy... in the meantime, the subsidies have all but dried up, with a boom-bust scenario for the entire sector as a result.

The free market is better at choosing the winners of tomorrow. If citizens or businesses do not want to spend money on activity ABC or investment XYZ, they probably have good reasons for their decisions. Perhaps they think they will get more for their money if they invest in D, E or F. If the government then takes tax money from those citizens or entrepreneurs in order to seduce them with subsidies into choosing ABC or XYZ, wealth will be lost. Why does the government think it is better placed than the individual citizen or entrepreneur to determine what is worthwhile and what not? Subsidies, tax deductions or exception regimes are effective ways of saying to citizens and businesses that "You don't know what's good for you; luckily the government does."

Governments seem to have become convinced over the years that they know better than individuals. Spending is higher now than ever before. The additional increase in government spending in the West is also striking (see illustration 28).

This increase illustrates that the government arrogates to itself more and more decision-making power at the expense of the sovereignty of every citizen or entrepreneur. Of every 100 euros spent in Belgium, the government spends 54 of them. By comparison: in 1960, it was only 30. The strong increase in government spending shows first and foremost that governments do not trust individuals and free markets. There is no other explanation for the fact that the government in Belgium, for example, has to be able to make decisions about more than half of all expenditures made in the country. Moreover, this policy is beginning to be counterproductive, contributing less and less growth. In spite of the particularly strong increase in the government's power to make decisions, our capacity to create wealth has deteriorated. The growth of productivity – our capacity to innovate and compete – has declined even further (see illustration 29).

It is striking how the increase in government spending has gone hand in hand with an increasing downshift in our innovation and growth engines. The most charitable interpretation of this evolution is that our capacity to create wealth has gone downhill, 'in spite of' the attempts of the government to ensure more growth. In this interpretation, there are probable external factors that have had a negative effect on growth which government expenditures have not been able to reverse. A more realistic interpretation is that the gradual increase in government spending has resulted in a decrease in our capacity to create wealth. By trying to assume an ever larger role

Illustration 28: **The government does more than ever...**
Source: *The Economist*, IMF Fiscal Monitor (April 2013)

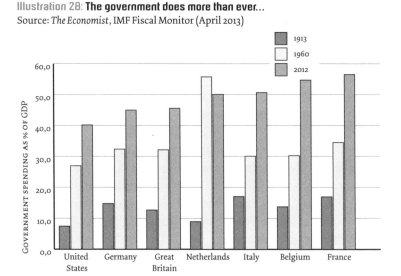

in the economy, the government has suppressed the most efficient manner of creating wealth: the free market.

INSTITUTIONS: GROWTH NEEDS FERTILE GROUND

Increasingly, the perception is growing that institutions are also very important in explaining the differences in growth from country to country. Institutions comprise a whole constituted by formal and informal rules, customs or habits within a society. It could be the degree to which caprice and corruption are controlled, the degree to which property rights are protected, the efficiency of the legal system or trust in government and institutions.

The economists Daron Acemoglu and James A. Robinson describe in *Why Nations Fail* how various institutions give rise to totally different outcomes. They distinguish between *extractive institutions* on the one hand and *inclusive institutions* on the other.

Illustration 29: **Our capacity for innovation is under stress.**
Source: OESO, StatExtracts

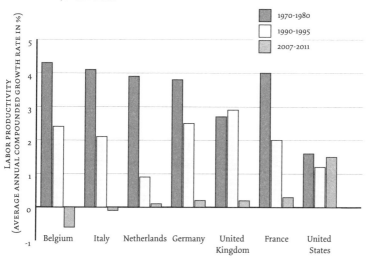

169

In the case of extractive institutions, the ruling class will attempt to consolidate its power using every means possible. This can range from personally controlling city corporations, demanding bribes for government contracts, granting monopolies to family members or political cronies or shifting government funds to tax shelters. A society in which caprice, corruption and a lack of transparency rule is a society in which an individual citizen or entrepreneur has no interest whatsoever in trying to get ahead in life. Neither by starting new business ventures, nor by investing, nor by competing, nor by innovating.

According to figures from the World Bank, in a country like Nigeria, for example, it is necessary to go through 13 different procedures in order to register property officially. This means 13 different stages at which one always runs the risk of having to pay a bribe. The total cost is usually in the neighborhood of 20% more than the property is actually worth. Because the official registration of property is made extraordinarily expensive in this way, many people choose to buy a piece of ground or a house without an 'official' registration. Because they cannot prove that the property in question really belongs to them as a result, they are twice as vulnerable. In the first place, they have no defense against someone who wants to take their property away. Certainly not if that party or person is supported by corrupt agents, police or judges. Moreover, it is impossible to use a 'non-official' property as collateral for a loan. For this reason it is nearly impossible to get a loan to start a new business or make an investment.

The ruling class, by contrast, finds itself at the receiving end of this system. They will do everything possible to maintain the system of extractive institutions. Growth, innovation and progress will be nipped in the bud whenever possible. In a society in which individual efforts and entrepreneurship are suffocated under the leaden blanket of caprice, corruption, violence or a biased legal system, citizens will lose all interest in getting ahead in life. Why invest in property if this will only encourage the ruling class to collect taxes on it?

Why start a business if the various state monopolies brook no competition? Why start a business of your own if you have to pay protection money, and the police and the judges will only help if bribed? Why send children to school if the best places in society are reserved for the family and political friends of the ruling class? The political and economic elites of many developing countries want to consolidate their power using any means necessary. A truly free market is a genuine threat to their supremacy (see also chapter 2). Consumers who can make their own choices form a threat to state monopolies and the wealth of the ruling families and political friends of the regime. Competition and innovation from new companies has the same effect.

Carlos Slim, for example, is the second richest man in the world and owes his fortune in part to these kinds of extractive institutions. He purchased the Mexican national telephone company Telmex from the government and was able – thanks to his political friends – to secure a virtual monopoly on telephone services. This is partly why he is so wealthy. The difference between him and the richest man in the world – the American Bill Gates – could hardly be greater. Gates started his own business from nothing in a competitive market and made his fortune with it. And even that does not make him above the law. Between 2001 and 2004, the American and European authorities fined his firm Microsoft for abusing its position as a monopoly. But even that would be unthinkable in a country with extractive institutions, like Mexico.

In essence, extractive institutions are the polar opposite of creative destruction. Creation would benefit the people, destruction would occur at the cost of the ruling class. By inhibiting freedom, innovation, and entrepreneurship, the political elite consolidates its own power at the expense of the entire population. Although extractive institutions are less of a problem for Western countries, the perception is growing that this is one of the most important obstacles to economic growth, progress and wealth in developing countries.

There are many obstacles to the growth of wealth. The two largest obstacles for the West are demography and massive public debt. The aging of the Japanese and European populations in particular is an obstacle that can hardly be avoided. We can try to contain its most far-reaching effects, but the aging of the population will be as fundamental a part of upcoming decades as the weather: it is advisable to bring along an umbrella if the sky is cloudy, but that won't stop it from raining.

The mountain of public debt in the West is largely of our own making. For the last couple of decades we have created a great deal of wealth through innovation, competition, and progress, but since the 1970s we have opted for wealth by installments. Today, we have a choice: give up wealth, or pay up.

The remaining stumbling blocks on the way to creating wealth seem much easier to remedy. In the West as in developing countries, it often comes down to the same pattern: a small group that tries to deny society as a whole the advantages of progress. Whether we are talking about monopolies, protectionism, interest groups, or extractive institutions: a small, well-defined group succeeds in having their own advantages paid for at the cost of decreasing wealth for all the rest.

SUBSIDIES CREATE LOSERS

Subsidies are a modern form of superstition. A superstition that finds that the government knows better than the market which industries, sectors, goods or services will be successful in the long run. According to the government, solar panels need subsidies "because they are not yet competitive." Wind turbines need subsidies because "they are still not yet competitive." The automobile industry needs subsidies "because it is not competitive right now." The same goes for nuclear energy as well. The only way nuclear energy can be profitable today is through indirect government subsidies. The largest of these is insurance against the risk of nuclear accident – something that would hardly be insurable in a free market. By taking on that risk, the government is in fact subsidizing nuclear energy at the cost of other forms of energy.

Why should the government be better placed than the market to know which sectors will be successful? The market unites the opinions, preferences and desires of millions of people. What better way to determine what works and what not?

From the perspective of their ideological preferences, politicians probably have an idea of which sectors or industries *ought* to be successful. Perhaps they dream of a world without nuclear power plants, filled with wind turbines and solar panels. Perhaps they dream of a world without large-scale agriculture, filled exclusively with small-scale, biological farms. Or perhaps they dream that the 'industry of the future' will establish itself in their own region. But this does not mean that they can simply conjure up that reality with subsidies.

Nevertheless, this is not to say that the government has no place in the process at all. In selecting the 'right' technology or the 'winning' sector of the future, everyone has his or her role to play – even the government. Its role consists in supporting basic and applied scientific research in every way possible. The role of scientists and engineers is to determine which technology or which solution works best, and to build on this knowledge. The role of the free market, finally, is to determine which of these technologies can also withstand the test of the market by convincing consumers.

In a free market, two competing technologies, products or businesses can fight it out between themselves as to who will receive the consumer's favor. They – and they alone – will be the ones who have to convince the consumer in terms of price, quality and service. Only the individual citizen and consumer is the ultimate referee for determining which product, which service or which technology is worthwhile. Why would a politician be better placed to make such choices? When politicians play favorites by means of subsidies, the entire playing field is distorted. The consumer will no longer choose solar panels because it's a good idea, but because a politician thinks it's a good idea. Nevertheless, subsidies are firmly entrenched in daily economic reality.

The European predilection for subsidies originated in the aftermath of the Second World War. An entire continent had to be rebuilt and an enormous population had to be fed. Subsidies for coal, steel and later agriculture were the best way to ensure the quick return of growth and wealth. The exceptional circumstances prevailing after the cataclysm argued in favor of greater interventionism on the part of the government. Since then, specific subsidies seem to have fused completely with the DNA of Europe and even that of the United States.

PAY ONCE, GET RIPPED OFF TWICE

The agricultural subsidies of the United States and Europe represent an injustice that is still being perpetrated against developing countries and Western consumers.

The combination of subsidies for domestic producers and what more or less amounts to a prohibition against competition for foreign producers is a hangman's noose for farmers from developing countries. A fictitious example reveals with stunning clarity how the consumer must pay twice. Imagine that a European farmer can grow tomatoes for three euros per kilogram and a Moroccan farmer – blessed with plenty of sun and cheap labor – for one euro per kilogram. By giving the European farmer subsidies, we can ensure that he brings his tomatoes to market for two euros per kilogram. In addition, there is a hefty import duty of 1.50 euros per kilogram on the Moroccan tomatoes, so that they will cost the European consumer 2.50 euros per kilogram. And behold, a miracle: the European consumer is offered European tomatoes in the supermarket that are 50 cents cheaper per kilogram than the 'more expensive' Moroccan variety. Even though, in reality, the Moroccan tomatoes cost only a third of the European tomatoes. The most surreal aspect of the operation is that it is financed by the consumers themselves. It is their tax money that makes this policy possible. Just imagine: you pay taxes so that your freedom of choice can be limited in an artificial way, and that you are thereby obliged to pay higher prices.

It is a policy that, in a very direct way, denies poor countries the chance to get richer. Although the poorest countries have received more favorable conditions for exporting to Europe for some time, they lose that advantage from the moment they graduate from 'dirt poor' to 'just poor'. The wealthy West offers the poorest countries a ladder with which to climb higher up, but after mounting the first two rungs they find that the next five have been broken underfoot.

CORPORATE WELFARE

Other examples of the negative effects of subsidies can be found in industrial policy. Although the ostensible purpose of many subsidies is to help sectors that are seen as promising, in practice this is often not the case. For every instance of a successful industrial policy, there are at least ten others that have failed.

Recent history is also strewn with examples of subsidized industries that eventually go under anyway – in spite of the subsidies. Throughout its death throes, and also because of its death throes, the Belgian shipbuilding sector received gigantic subsidies. Until it was clear to everyone that it could no longer be saved, at which point the entire sector inevitably sank. The same thing happened with the coal mines. There, too, enormous sums were swallowed up by subsidies that were meant to shore up an unprofitable industry. And we haven't even started on Belgium's former national airline, the steel industry, or the automobile sector. All subsidies in a bottomless pit: they kept the sector afloat and, at the same time, created the illusion of added value and economic activity so that the sector in question was completely anaesthetized to economic reality. In practice, subsidies often go to the companies, projects, technologies or sectors of politically and socially well-connected individuals, companies or sectors. Once things begin to go wrong with the projects or industries involved, the government is very poorly placed to judge the degree to which additional subsidies are still justified. In the first place, they probably have skin in the game – their own credibility is at stake, but they still don't feel too concerned about the financial means involved. First and foremost, it is not about their own personal means, but those of the taxpayer. Moreover, as mentioned above, it is often the very industrialists, interest groups, or labor unions who have the politician's attention, and not the taxpayer who has to finance the whole operation.

The expression *corporate welfare* sums up this problem perfectly: industries that receive welfare benefits. These industries and their political protectors all have 1,001 reasons to justify why they will certainly need subsidies. The basic principle is, nevertheless, quite simple: if it's not viable without subsidies, it's not viable at all. Period.

MAKE IT EASIER FOR THE MARKET

Every attempt by the government to choose the industrial winners is all too often doomed to failure. To repeat: why should the government be better placed to do this than the market – that collection of billions of individual people with all their individual needs and desires?

Subsidies are the ultimate form of pedantry. The government that determines how the future ought to look – against the will of the citizen. What is the chance that the government would have discovered Bill Gates from Microsoft, Steve Jobs from Apple, Mark Zuckerberg from Facebook or Sergey Brin from Google while they were working in their garages or dorm rooms and recognized them as the future of technology, and their ideas as the technology of the future?

The government is not best placed for distinguishing the technologies and ideas of the future. What can the government do, then? Should it just sit by unoccupied and watch until progress, technology, innovation, growth and jobs just appear out of nowhere? Of course not! The government is in the best position to ensure good preconditions for the creation of wealth: innovation, basic and applied research, entrepreneurship and the free market. In concrete terms, these preconditions consist of outstanding education, an attractive environment for research and development, effective patent protection, attractive incentives for risk capital, sound bankruptcy laws, an efficient judiciary for enforcing contracts, free trade and, of course, the guarantee of a free market.

Thus, the government has an essential role in making wealth possible. That role consists primarily in creating the right environmental factors for making competition and innovation possible. It is a dangerous illusion to believe that a government can conjure up wealth by handing out subsidies. Progress and innovation are not *created* by the government and subsidies. Progress and innovation *come into existence,* thanks to the free market and competition.

CHAPTER 10

The road to prosperity

"Cynicism masquerades as wisdom, but it is the farthest thing from it. Because cynics don't learn anything. Because cynicism is a self-imposed blindness, a rejection of the world because we are afraid it will hurt us or disappoint us. Cynics always say no. But saying 'yes' begins things. Saying 'yes' is how things grow. Saying 'yes' leads to knowledge. 'Yes' is for young people. So for as long as you have the strength to, say 'yes'." — **Stephen Colbert**, American actor, comedian, and author (°1964)

"You'll always miss 100% of the shots you don't take." — **Wayne Gretzky**, retired Canadian ice hockey player, considered the best of all time (°1961)

"Give me a challenge, and I'll meet it with joy … The future doesn't belong to the fainthearted; it belongs to the brave." — **Ronald Reagan (1911-2004)**, former president of the United States of America (1981-1989)

"The one thing modern democracy will not bear without cracking is the … substantial lowering of the standards of living in peacetime or even prolonged stationariness of its economic conditions." — **Friedrich Hayek**

"A movement whose main promise is the relief from responsibility cannot but be antimoral in its effect." — **Friedrich Hayek**

Belief in free markets is under pressure today. In Belgium and in Europe, the prevailing attitude now is one of disappointment in an economy that no longer seems to succeed in creating progress and wealth.

The financial crisis of 2008 transitioned seamlessly into an economic crisis that only ended in 2009. For the first time since the end of the Second World War, the world economy produced less than the year before. While the rest of the world – Asia, Africa, Latin America and the United States – has since resumed economic growth, Europe is still mired in quicksand. Apart from the after effects of too much debt, the financial-economic crisis of 2008-2009 exposed fundamental weaknesses in the construction of the monetary union. Repairing these weaknesses and reducing debt costs us wealth today.

THE BANKS ARE AT FAULT

In spite of all that, the combination of financial crisis, weak growth and institutional bungling also provokes two other reactions. The first reaction is to attribute all our current problems to the bank crisis – more specifically to the banks and the bankers themselves. Weren't they the ones who had to be bailed out, because they were the ones taking too many risks?

This question is perfectly justified. Of course they will not get off scot-free. Of course far too many risks were taken when things were still going well and there seemed to be no end to the great big money fest. Of course the financial sector played an important part in the collective build-up of debt in the West over the past few decades. But families, businesses, and governments have amassed debts on a permanent basis over the last few decades in order to create the illusion of growth. Whether we're talking about a business debt, an obligation, a mortgage or government debt: it's all money that has been spent with nothing to back it up. As explained earlier: debt is a glimpse of wealth that has yet to be earned. Of course the banks were involved. Just as the fuse box stands between incoming electricity on one side and all the household appliances on the other. When too much electricity comes in – or when too many demands are placed on the system – the fuses blow.

But this does not mean that an exclusive focus on the financial sector is the solution to our current problems. The bank crisis was a symptom of a growth pattern that was too reliant on the creation of debts and not reliant enough on the creation of wealth.

THE FREE MARKET IS AT FAULT

The second reaction to the lack of growth is increasing disapproval of the free market. Isn't it the rampant free market and its focus on self-interest that has caused the current malaise? Isn't it the free market and competition that result in massive lay-offs and unemployment? Don't we need to impose limits on the market?

There's a good chance that the average Indonesian, Brazilian or Chinese is not at all that negative when it comes to the free market. For them, the unprecedented growth of health, wealth and standards of living are precisely thanks to freedom, the free market and free trade. Better yet: many developing countries today probably even have too little of the free market! The degree to which governments or political elites in developing countries try to hold back the free market is telling with respect to how much they and their friends stand to lose personally.

Would the average Mexican really be worse off if the free market enabled him to choose which telephone company to use? Would an African farmer sink further into poverty if Europe really chose the free market and stopped subsidizing its own agriculture? Would the average Nigerian mourn if he could register his property without bribes, so that he could start his own business? Wouldn't an average Congolese farmer like to have a tractor without worrying that he might lose it for whatever reason?

For the majority of the world economy today, more free market is a pipe dream. To be able to decide when and where to come and go, what to buy and what to sell. Without government interference. Without political elites who choose their own financial and economic interests or those of their friends above the interests of society at large.

Apparently, Europeans seem to be the ones most likely to reject the free market. This expresses itself in a number of ways. One of them is an increasing choice in favor of protectionism as a way of protecting citizens and companies from 'murderous' competition with other countries. That citizens are the ones who reap the benefits of that 'murderous' competition in the form of greater freedom of choice and lower prices is often conveniently forgotten.

PESSIMISM IS FASHIONABLE

The increasing call for budgetary stimulus, large-scale 'action plans for growth', additional redistribution of wealth or all sorts of government intervention is reinforced by a self-reinforcing pessimism.

Everyone would like to be remembered. Most people would like to be remembered above all by their family and friends, while other people have ambitions of going down in history. Economists, prognosticators and analysts, are no different to other mortals in this respect. They too would like to be remembered for a prediction they made. There is a simple rule of thumb, however, that says it's easier to be remembered when you predict a disaster than when you predict that everything will turn out all right. Take the weatherman, for example. A weatherman who correctly predicts a beautiful summer's day is already forgotten three days later. Everybody is at the beach or having a barbecue and is mostly glad that the weather's nice. A weatherman who incorrectly predicts a beautiful summer's day is also forgotten three days later. The weather is bad, people are complaining about weathermen and their inability to make predictions, but life goes on. Conclusion: predicting beautiful weather is no way to be remembered for eternity.

Now let's see what we can do with bad weather. A weatherman predicts a storm of biblical proportions. If the storm never arrives, the weatherman is once again forgotten after three days. People still talk about the prediction over the barbecue, but the dreaded deluge and 'hailstones the size of tennis balls' are soon forgotten. Finally, let's look at one last scenario. the weatherman again predicts a storm of biblical proportions, hailstones and all, and to top it off a plague of locusts as well. This time he's right and his prediction comes true. Frightened people huddle in their homes and suffer through the violence of nature. The weatherman, by contrast, is assured of lasting fame as the prophet of the Apocalypse…

"An optimist is a poorly informed pessimist." That tends to be the attitude of the public whenever the future of Belgium or Europe is the subject of discussion. Today, a great many prognosticators have the inclination to be pessimistic or negative. Anyone who predicts the total collapse of the monetary union is rarely asked – or not asked at all – to provide an argument or reasoning. Those who say with certainty that we are all heading towards poverty or bankruptcy are easily believed. A negative attitude is already sufficient for being found credible. By contrast, those who say that we will experience a turnaround, and that we have everything at our disposal to climb out of the current malaise, is at best viewed as misguided and at worst gullible.

This does not mean that there is no reason for healthy skepticism or critical reflection. It certainly doesn't mean that gullibility is recommendable. The challenges are certainly immense. We are looking at a concurrent financial, economic, institutional, demographic and social crisis. Moreover, there is no *deus ex machina* that will swoop down and provide a miraculous answer to all our problems. There is no bottle of miracle solutions we can uncork. But concluding from all this that the Occident is heading towards inevitable implosion is going a bit too far.

There really is a lot at stake. Nothing is more corrosive than a lack of growth and hope. Without growth, hope disappears. Hope for greater wealth and hope for a better life. Without hope, no one feels called to launch new enterprises, stick their neck out or show ambition. In a society that no longer grows, individual success, ambition, and progress increasingly arouse envy. A phenomenon like the so-called 'millionaire tax' in France is a perfect illustration of how far things have gone. A society that finds such a 'tax on success' normal is no longer interested in wealth, ambition or progress.

An economy without hope, without growth and without ambition will slowly but surely evolve towards a permanent state of lethargy. The individual will increasingly have to yield to the collective on many different levels. An unemployment problem will be increasingly solved by subsidies or by the redistribution of existing work, and not by placing more responsibility on the shoulders of the unemployed themselves. Sectors experiencing difficulties will have easier access to financial support, subsidies or special tax regimes than in the past, instead of taking responsibility themselves. Increased unemployment is, after all, a losing proposition politically. Solidarity will come first. Responsibility will become less and less important.

We are sliding into a society in which individual success is subordinate to an ideal image of redistribution. In which lowering standards is more important than excelling. In which taking risks is discouraged and the risk-free is promulgated. In which the responsibility of the individual is minimized and that of society is maximized.

In a society in which 'The government!' is the answer to all questions, there is no longer room for the individual. In such an environment, it is easy to imagine that the most creative, the most enterprising or the most successful people will seek out greener pastures. That is the major paradox of today. Now that we need growth, risk, entrepreneurship and economic revolution, political and social readiness to take the necessary steps is waning.

This problem is depicted clearly in illustration 30. Confidence is shown on the vertical axis. Economic growth is on the horizontal axis. Confidence must be seen in a broader sense than just the results of a monthly survey on consumer and producer confidence. It is also about confidence in the future, readiness to invest or to undertake new enterprises. It is the social 'appetite' for going all out and in fact determines a society's robustness. Those who have confidence in the future can withstand a few hard knocks.

Economic growth should also be seen in a broader sense than just the most recent quarterly growth figures of the gross domestic product. It is an economy's potential for growth, its capacity for innovation and creating wealth. In the illustration this produces four quadrants.

Quadrant I represents *immobilism*. This is the phase in which a large part of Europe finds itself today. There is no growth and little hope

Illustration 30: **Growth and confidence in the four corners of the world**

Source: Ignace Van Doorselaere

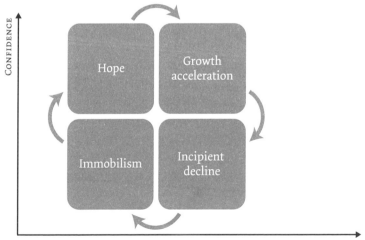

of improvement. Nobody moves, people no longer take initiatives and no one dares to launch new enterprises any more. This is also the only quadrant in which people consider moving. To a place where there is either more hope or more growth, and preferably both at the same time. For example: Spaniards who emigrate to Latin America or Germany, or Portuguese who look for work in Angola or Brazil. Nor is Belgium immune to this sort of movement. Moreover, migrations of this kind threaten to reinforce the downward spiral even further. When the most creative, most active, most enterprising and highest earning people from a society look for greener pastures, the decrease in wealth and income tax revenues for the government is much greater than the decrease in the total population. If all the well-educated Spanish engineers were to leave the country tomorrow and go to work in Germany or the United States, it will be much more difficult for the Spanish government to make ends meet. They no longer have a large portion of tax revenues and created wealth, while the students, unemployed and people of retirement age who rely on the government have not left the country.

Quadrant II represents *hope*: a combination of low growth and increasing confidence. There is visible progress, but it still hasn't translated into an increase in growth. The seeds of new growth are found here. The United States is currently in this quadrant. The economy has not completely recovered its former glory, but the confidence of citizens and entrepreneurs is improving. Whatever the case may be, this is the quadrant where Europe needs to go now. Europe can model itself after the United States, but let's be honest. American society has at its disposal a unique, inborn resilience and optimism that made the transition to quadrant II much easier.

Quadrant III is *growth acceleration* and represents a combination of extreme confidence in the future and a high degree of progress and economic growth. In this quadrant we find most *emerging markets*. If they look in the rear-view mirror for a moment, they will realize that they have made immense progress on all levels over the last two decades. Life expectancy, risk of poverty, food supply and wealth have all evolved in the right direction – and moreover, much faster than in the West. Rapid growth shores up hope and perpetuates confidence in the future. Confidence in the future encourages entrepreneurship, innovation and competition and, in this way, perpetuates growth. The last time Belgium found itself in such a state must have been in the 1950s and 1960s. At the time there was a tangible feeling of economic growth and progress in the air. A feeling that everything was possible and that everyone was getting ahead.

Quadrant IV is the quadrant of incipient decline: there is still growth, but confidence is beginning to falter. Innovation is more difficult, cartels or monopolies retard growth, interest groups begin to demand advantages that the economy cannot support... Well-being has caught up with wealth. Better yet: the demand for well-being seems to increase faster than the wealth needed to finance it.

Emerging markets are hard at work paving the way toward the future and they are advancing with lightning speed on all levels. They are also catching up with us at lightning speed. Since the fall of the Berlin Wall and the collapse of the Soviet Union, they have chosen more freedom, more free trade and more free market. This has served them well, as is evident from illustration 31. It shows how wealth per capita has developed in different regions. Between 1975 and 1990, the average wealth in a country like Belgium tripled. Between 1990 and 2010, the total wealth increased by only 50%. For the European Union as a whole, we see the same phenomenon. Between 1975 and 1990, the average wealth increased at least 365%. In the last twenty years, it increased by less than 70%. In spite of the debt-financed growth of the last two decades, our capacity to create wealth has thus declined.

The poorest countries, by contrast – thanks to freedom, free trade and the free market – have made a great leap forward. Their affluence over the last two decades has increased much faster than in the period before. In East Asian developing countries, for example, wealth per inhabitant doubled between 1975 and 1990. Between 1990 and 2010, however, it increased fivefold. The poorest countries are still often the least free countries today, have the most restrictions on private property and the most corrupt or least free market.

However, it is their evolution towards freedom – on all levels – that has brought about the major reversal.

It is to be expected that developing countries and emerging markets will continue to overtake the West in the years to come. The big problem today is in Europe, where the engine of growth seems to have stalled and a feverish search is on for new, magic ways to generate growth and wealth again.

INGREDIENTS FOR GROWTH

It would be a capital mistake if, as a reaction to the current crisis, we were to turn away from the free market, competition and progress. If we were to withdraw into ourselves and reject globalization. If we were to intervene even more in market forces: by introducing minimum or maximum prices, by using subsidies to guide people's choices, by redistributing work, by selecting the 'industries of the future', by choosing the redistribution of wealth over growth.

Illustration 31: **Growth of wealth per inhabitant**
Source: World Bank

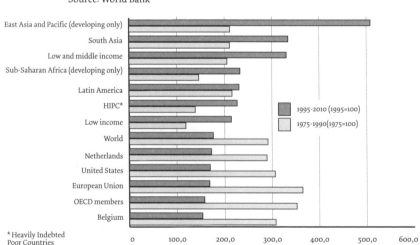

* Heavily Indebted
Poor Countries

188

Certainly in these uncertain economic times, the government's temptation to determine how money is spent and where progress will come from must be great.

Contrary to what some people think, the government does not create growth and wealth. They are generated when every citizen takes his or her own responsibility. In short, the solution consists in giving individual citizens more choices and more freedom. With more and better education, fewer subsidies to influence people's behavior and lower, less complicated taxes, it will be possible for wealth to arise and flourish.

Here are the five main priorities:

» First the growth of wealth, only then well-being.
» Invest everything in education, training and research.
» Freedom and the free market are the norm, not the exception.
» What is not viable without subsidies is not viable at all.
» Guarantee a minimum income and a flat tax.

1 First the growth of wealth, only then well-being

The growth of wealth must have top priority. When the economy grows, more people will find a job. When the economy grows, the gap in the budget will fix itself. When the economy grows, everyone gets ahead. When the economy grows, everyone can share in the wealth more easily.

Wealth is not created, it comes into being. The word 'creation' gives rise to the illusion that jobs or wealth can be developed according to some fixed process. That if one pushes the right buttons, wealth and jobs will come into existence. Better yet: that the government can perhaps push those buttons more efficiently than anyone else so that a maximum amount of wealth and jobs can be created. Nothing could be further from the truth. Wealth comes into being when citizens and businesses get the chance to be creative, have the freedom to launch new enterprises and are encouraged to be successful. Wealth and jobs come into being when citizens and entrepreneurs can demand the best of themselves. Wealth and jobs are a by-product of citizens and entrepreneurs who are encouraged to pursue their enlightened self-interest.

The redistribution of wealth will not guarantee more wealth. In the wealthiest continent in the world, in the country with the greatest income equality, the lack of redistribution is increasingly offered up as *the* problem of our age. Redistribution ... redistributing wealth is not the answer to the fact that wealth is no longer growing.

If we want everyone to make progress, we will have to focus not on redistribution, but on the growth of wealth. In recent decades, however, redistribution has become second nature. We have all redistributed to the max – through the increase in government debt, we have even borrowed from future generations. The growth of wealth that is necessary for its redistribution is under enormous stress. The call for more redistribution threatens, in this way, to cut off the very branch – the creation of wealth – on which it sits. The redistribution of wealth is a sign of civilization; too much redistribution is the end of wealth.

2 Invest everything in education, training and research

Labor is everything, training is everything. Everything that we have built up during the spectacular growth spurt of the last two centuries comes down to labor. More labor, better-educated labor and more productive labor.

The value of an apple consists entirely of the labor carried out by the person who plucked it. If that person used a tractor, for example, the write-off of the farming equipment is calculated into the selling price of the apple. The equipment itself is the result of a design by engineers and tool specialists: mental work, thus. Assembling the tractor is carried out through the efforts of laborers. The electricity they need to do so is a product of the labor of more engineers, this time in nuclear physics, as well as the employees who service the high voltage lines, and so forth. And we're still only talking about an apple.

Now let's look at the other end of the value spectrum: a smartphone. The design of its packaging, screen, apps and functions is the work of engineers, product designers and graphic designers. The parts themselves come from the labor of employees in Korea or China. The raw materials for the product come from laborers in the chemical industry or copper mines. Its transport is ensured by the labor of seamen, stevedores, truck drivers and express delivery services along every step of the way. The final sale relies on display designers and salespeople who know their merchandise. It is the sum total of all the labor that determines the added value of a product, service or economic activity.

Only human beings add value. Their exertions alone ensure progress. Everything we cultivate, build or exploit on this planet was essentially already on this planet thousands of years ago. All the oil, copper, gold, iron and coal that happens to be buried in the ground does not make us wealthier. Everything that happens to grow on our property does not make us wealthier. It is what people do with these things that creates added value and wealth. It is not the cultivation of coffee beans that yields the greatest added value, but their roasting, grinding, packaging and marketing. It is not plucking olives that will yield the greatest added value, but the creation and marketing of a wide variety of olive oils that makes the difference. It is not the assembly of glass, microchips and switches that yields the most added value, but the marketing of a concept, such as a smartphone. Whether it is agricultural labor, an invention in the laboratory, the assembly of a tractor or the invention of a more efficient production process: added value is provided by people.

The only way to create wealth is to do 'things' better than we do today. That is innovation, and it leads to progress. We can only do this if we make education, ongoing instruction and research and development a top priority. We are no longer engaged in a race to the bottom for the lowest wages, but a race to the top. A race to the top for the best students, the best-educated employees and the smartest inventors. The more we think, the better we think, the more we invent and the more we innovate, the more wealth we cause to come into being. Therefore this must be the top priority.

It is not as if our technological advantage over emerging markets or even over developing countries is guaranteed for eternity. Stories about the hundreds of thousands of engineers who graduate in China, data centers in India and highly educated Asians are a clear signal that we will only be able to make our wealth grow if we invest more in education, research and development and constant training. Children of uneducated parents do not receive enough education themselves. Children of well-educated parents are also well educated. Children of well-educated parents become rocket scientists... Education, training and research are the only elements we need in this race to the top, in this race to more wealth.

3 Freedom and the free market are the norm, not the exception

As we have already seen, the free market is the best guarantee of creating as much wealth possible for as many people possible. Inhibiting the free market inevitably inhibits the creation of wealth. We have no use for fantastic innovations if they run aground in a market that is not free. Even today and in Western societies, the free market – and hence the coming into being of wealth – is undermined in a number of ways.

» Automatically allowing wages to increase on the basis of seniority – the number of years worked – is not free market. In a free market, wages would be determined by the value added or the productivity of the employee. Whether she had been working for the company three months, three years or three decades: she who adds the most value deserves to earn the most.

» Arranging wage agreements for an entire economy or an entire sector at one go is not free market. It denies individual companies and individual employees the right to come to a mutual agreement about what they consider appropriate compensation.

» Limiting compensation or bonuses within particular sectors is not free market. Agreements about wages, premiums, raises or bonuses are agreements between employees and employers.

» Rescuing particular sectors that are threatening to go under on account of their apparent social or economic importance is not free market. In a free market, fear of bankruptcy keeps companies on their toes. If the risk of bankruptcy is excluded from the outset – by the government, for example – it amounts to giving companies a subsidy in the form of a life insurance policy, as it were. Whether baker, automobile assembly worker or financial institution, the laws of the free market hold for everyone.

» The arbitrary raising of minimum wages or automatic indexing of wages generally does not add wealth. The only way to ensure wealth is to strive for higher productivity. The only way to achieve higher productivity and wealth is to provide better education, ongoing training and research and development.

» Prohibiting clearances outside preset clearance periods is not free market. Individual businesses should be able to compete with one another year round. Anyone who wants to hold monthly clearances should be able to do so. Limiting clearance periods places the consumer at a disadvantage.

» Prohibiting or limiting opening hours for supermarkets is not free market. Anyone who wants to keep a supermarket open 24/7 should have the right to do so. Citizens will decide whether such a project is viable or not.

» Prohibiting or limiting foreign architects, engineers, pharmacists, doctors and the like who come here to work is not free market. Each company individually has to decide whether unfamiliarity with the language weighs too heavily against eventual advantages in terms of cost.

The free market exists to give everyone the chance to get ahead, not to enable limited groups to continue reinforcing what they feel to be their inherent rights. A market that is not free wastes wealth.

4 What is not viable without subsidies is not viable at all

Today, there are many sectors that receive subsidies from the government. Support from the government is not wrong in and of itself, as long as that support is used for education, training, innovation or research and development. This is where the top priority should lie in the granting of government support. Alas, subsidies all too often go to old industries that have stubbornly refused to keep up with the times. In Belgium, the railways, shipbuilding industry, steel sector and coalmines are all good examples. Moreover, subsidies all too often go to the pet projects of politicians who find their own opinion more important than that of the free market. A few examples include nuclear energy, solar panels, buses that run on natural gas, tourism and culture. Subsidies are all too often granted to politically friendly sectors that detest the free market and therefore need protection from their competitors.

There is often a much more efficient and much more effective system of keeping businesses sharp and allowing them to innovate. That system is called 'the free market'. No one gave Apple subsidies to bring a groundbreaking design like the iPhone on the market, and in this way, practically bring a company like Nokia to its knees. No one gave BMW subsidies for spectacularly increasing their market share with more attractive models and more energy-efficient engines.

Subsidies try to direct the choices of the consumer and citizen or even to curtail their choices. European agricultural subsidies are a case in point. The combination of agricultural subsidies for domestic products and import duties on foreign competitors limits the choice of European consumers and forces them to pay higher prices than would be the case in a truly competitive market.

The free market is the best way to allow companies to innovate. Those who don't make it, disappear. Those who can convince consumers on the basis of price, quality, and service, will be richly rewarded. The best way to wring the neck of the selection mechanism is to hand out subsidies. Subsidies make businesses lazy. Competition keeps companies sharp.

5 Guarantee a minimum income and a flat tax

Taxes are necessary. The taxes every citizen pays are the price of our civilization. It is the price we pay so that the government can keep order, enforce contracts and provide public infrastructure. All of these elements are necessary so that wealth can come into existence. Today's heavy tax burden and complex tax system – in most parts of Europe, at any rate – have grown into an obstacle that prevents wealth from coming into being to the degree that it otherwise might.

The current tax system in Belgium, for example, reflects in the first place a great distrust on the part of the government for the choices and capacity for judgment of the individual citizen. Of every 100 euros that are spent in Belgium, the government spends more than half. Of all the wealth that comes into being, citizens can decide on the allocation of less than half.

The country's sizable tax burden discourages the creation of wealth, the complexity of the taxes encourages fraud and arbitrary practices, and the paternalistic stance of tax law has resulted in a gigantic tangle of premiums, subsidies and concessions.

There is, however, one way to reform the tax system into a system that is not only more just, but that also encourages the creation of wealth and discourages fraud. A system in which the citizen receives far more freedom, and in which social solidarity is nevertheless preserved. That system is a flat tax in combination with a minimum income.

A flat tax means that every euro earned is subject to the same amount of tax. This is not presently the case. A euro today that is earned by labor is, on average, taxed more heavily than a euro deriving from interest or capital. Moreover, a euro earned by someone who earns a great deal is taxed at a higher rate than a euro earned by someone who earns very little. A flat tax would introduce a single tax rate.

At the same time, all deductions would have to be eliminated or at least heavily reduced. Deductions, special tax regimes and exceptional rates are highly inefficient. In Belgium alone, tax law is one vast network of Byzantine regulations that a human being cannot possibly hope to navigate. Correction: that a human being with a well-paid financial advisor can navigate with a modicum of success, but an average citizen cannot. With every new deduction, subsidy or concession, the government seeks to control the behavior of citizens or companies. In practice, however, it is an enormous waste of time, energy and money that is difficult to administer.

Eliminating deductions would not only increase efficiency, it would also limit the interference of the government in the private choices of citizens and companies. This in itself would already increase wealth. Those who want to buy solar panels can decide for themselves and do not need anyone to hold their hand – in the form of a tax deduction, for example. Those who want to take the train to work or drive their car can decide themselves, and not have the 'right' choice imposed on them. The same goes for a company that wants to invest or do business internationally. Fewer deductions would also exclude the tendency towards fiscal optimization behavior: decisions would be made because they are interesting, not because they offer tax advantages.

Finally, a guaranteed minimum income is in itself a good idea. It is a regular income – the same amount for everyone – that everyone receives regardless of whether he or she works. There is nothing wrong with having solidarity with other people; indeed, our ability to share wealth is what makes us human. It is only that the intricate complexity of that solidarity today encourages abuse, inactivity, and great loss of wealth. Belgium – and Europe – is wealthy enough to provide each of its citizens with a minimum income regardless of activity, efforts or value added. Those who decide to remain inactive on that income have the right to do so. Those who wish to supplement that income with work or entrepreneurship also have the right to do so, without losing their minimum income.

The combination of a flat tax and a guaranteed minimum income meets all the conditions for once again generating more wealth...

» **The flat tax encourages enterprise and the creation of wealth:** every euro earned is taxed equally, regardless of how much you earn. From the first euro earned, you pay taxes. No complicated income ceilings, no different treatment for different sorts of income, no proliferation of deductions. Every euro is taxed equally.

» **The guaranteed minimum income encourages work:** everyone receives a minimum income, whether he works or not. The advantage is that working brings in money from the first hour worked. When an unskilled person accepts a job today and receives wages, he automatically loses his welfare benefits. Ultimately, it is possible that an entire month of work brings in only a few euros more than inactivity. This would not be the case with a minimum income. If the minimum income is acquired, it is maintained even when someone works for only a week. Someone who works one week per month will have more than someone who doesn't work at all. That is not the case in today's system. The guaranteed minimum income is a ladder to wealth with a very low bottom rung.

» **The guaranteed minimum income encourages freedom:** those who receive a minimum income can decide to stop working temporarily and go back to school. In this way, lifelong learning and education are stimulated. A minimum income can also encourage people to try their hand as an entrepreneur. Launching a new enterprise today often frightens people off because the choice is binary. Either you have the certainty of an income as an employee or welfare benefits from unemployment, or you have no certainty at all and sole responsibility as an entrepreneur. Those who seek financial support for a new enterprise or who want to go back to school temporarily get lost in an intricate tangle of systems, premiums, concessions, exemptions and all manner of compensations. A minimum income would make these things a lot easier.

» **The flat tax discourages fiscal optimization behavior and creates wealth:** fiscal optimization behavior is a particularly expensive, time-consuming inefficient and scarcely ethical pastime. Those who can afford the most expensive tax accountants or lawyers can reduce their tax burdens the most. A particularly complex tax code and an increasingly fat tax return may create more work for all sorts of advisors, tax accountants and specialists, but they do not in any way generate wealth. A system of flat tax – without deductions and without subsidies – will cause this entire cottage industry of advisors to melt away like snow in the sun.

» **The strongest shoulders bear the heaviest burdens:** someone who earns 1,000 euros bears twice the burden of someone who earns 500. The biggest earners will still pay the most taxes.

» **Everybody equal before the law:** it does not matter whether an income is acquired through labor, capital, rent or interest – every euro is taxed equally. In this way, optimizing income depending on origin and discouraging labor at the cost of investment will disappear. All ways of creating wealth are taxed equally.

» **Administration will be much cheaper:** administering and collecting the taxes generated by a flat tax will also be much cheaper. No more thousands of tax inspectors who have to check myriads of deductions or verify scads of supporting documents. Here the government can realize huge savings.

» **Fraud will melt like snow in the sun:** a simple tax system discourages fraud. If deductions no longer exist, the possibilities for submitting falsified tax returns diminish dramatically. Moreover, a lower tax rate means that fraud is no longer worth the trouble. Only when tax rates are unjustly high does the inclination toward fraudulence arise.

» **Citizens decide, not the government:** without deductions, concessions, tax credits or subsidies, everyone can decide for themselves what to do with their money. Citizens may decide for themselves whether to buy shares or save, buy a house or a vintage car, install solar panels or live a more luxurious lifestyle. It is the citizen who decides what is best, not the government.

OPTIMISM...

In addition to the five ingredients described above, there is one crucial element that we will need in any event – and in every scenario. That element is optimism. A more central role for the individual and a background role for the government go directly against the tendency of the last few decades. A political and social shift of this nature cannot be implemented just like that – one, two, three. There will be a great deal of resistance. Especially from those who have a vested interest in maintaining the status quo. Politics, institutions and lobby groups will resist a shift towards more power for the individual citizen. They will use all their power to resist the idea that the citizen is able to shape his or her own fate. They will fight back with the notion that poor, helpless citizens must be protected against globalization, against the free market and even against themselves.

This is not the case. A government whose most important task consists in allowing people to evade their own responsibilities does no one a service. The larger the government, the more it mistrusts the ability of citizens to shape their own lives and to make their own choices. Only a government that deliberately takes that ability away from people makes them truly helpless.

It will require great change in order to place the social system's center of gravity closer to citizens once again, to make the market freer, and to work against interest groups and the defenders of complexity, and paternalism. This is why optimism is necessary. Optimism concerning the capacities of each individual citizen. Optimism with respect to the possibilities of technology and science. Optimism when faced with each citizen's hunger for progress. Optimism about the possibilities giving each citizen to make his or her own choices. Optimism that the future will be freer for everyone.

Pessimists are all too often right. Real change, however, will only come from optimists.

Conversation with a growth pessimist

Unfortunately, there are far too many growth pessimists today. People who see the free market as a problem and not a solution. People who are overwhelmed by the steady stream of negative news about society, economy and planet. People who assume that it will only get worse. People who think our hands need holding so we don't head off in the wrong direction.

For them I offer the step-by-step plan below. A crash course in optimism with respect to the free market and progress...

What is actually the difference between 'the market' and 'the free market'?

A market is any physical or virtual place where goods, services, ideas or labor are exchanged. The free market is the ideal to be pursued.

This means: an environment in which people can trade with one another freely, without compulsion. An environment without subsidies. An environment without trade restrictions. An environment without import duties. An environment without monopolies or market power. An environment without political favoritism or corruption. In short, an environment in which only supply, demand and price play a role in the transactions between citizens.

In reality, the market is seldom actually free because the conditions outlined above are rarely met.

» Someone who obtains a monopoly on telecommunications thanks to their good connections with the leading political class operates within a market. But it is not a free market.
» Someone who receives a job contract thanks to connections within the company got that contract in a job market. But it is not a free market.
» A company that goes under because it has to go head to head with a subsidized competitor goes under in a market. But it is not a free market.

» Wages that are automatically raised on account of higher prices or higher inflation are raised in a market. But it is not a free market.
» Minimum wages that are established beforehand – regardless of qualifications or abilities – are paid in a market. But it is not a free market.

Don't defenders of the free market just want as little regulation as possible? They would rather have no rules at all.

Absolutely not. A market without rules and without regulation is not a free market. The government has a monopoly on enforcing contracts, but also on laying down the rules of play. A free market can only work when there are rules to which everyone must adhere. Pollution, fraud, tax evasion, monopoly forming, etc. are not consequences of the free market. They make it more difficult to have a free market.

Doesn't the free market result in more poverty and inequality?

Since the beginning of human history there has never been so much rapid progress as in the 20th century, the century in which freedom and the free market have resulted in a great leap forward for the world population.

Poverty and child mortality have declined spectacularly, life expectancy has doubled and literacy has increased. Moreover, progress and democratization go hand in hand. In 1900, 12% of the world population lived in a democracy; today that figure is already 64%.

The free market is certainly responsible for child labor.

Child labor is unfortunately a phenomenon that is older than the free market or the beginning of industrialization. Today, it is generally found in the poorest and least developed countries in the world. Only an increase in wealth can eradicate child labor. That was also the pattern during the industrial revolution in the West. The more complex and mechanized production processes became, the less child labor – with its low productivity – was able to add value. It was an intense rise in productivity and increase in wealth that helped eliminate child labor in the Western world.

This is precisely the formula that is needed in the poorest countries. A free market that gives them access to wealthy markets in the West, so that they can make real progress. In the long run this is the only solution for reducing poverty and ending child labor.

Ok then, no child labor and no poverty. But isn't the free market primarily responsible for all that environmental pollution?
Environmental pollution, overfishing, CO_2 emissions ... these things are the result of too little free market. A free market assumes that everyone has property rights for what he or she deals in. Selling a stolen car is a transaction on the free market, but doesn't add wealth.

The problem is that air, environment and climate don't belong to anybody. No one owns them, so no one feels compelled to take care of them. Different citizens or companies will never take the effects on someone else's property (air, climate, ocean) into account. This is an area in which government intervention is necessary.

The government is therefore in the best position to take these property rights into account. It can do so by charging duties for pollution, levying an environmental tax, setting up a market in emission rights, managing fishing permits, and other such useful measures.

Taking these externalities into account is also one of the necessary conditions for a properly functioning free market.

Whatever the case, the free market causes competition. Competition is bad.
Competition goes with the free market like night follows day: one can't exist without the other. Competition ensures that consumers always have access to the greatest possible supply at the most

attractive prices. It ensures that entrepreneurs and companies put their best foot forward and continue to invest effort in innovation.

The greatest victim of a lack of competition is always the consumer. Whenever competition is placed under restraint, or when suppliers make agreements among themselves to compete less, the consumer is always the dupe, especially the poorest consumers. It is precisely for these consumers that greater supply, more choice, and lower prices make the most difference.

We don't really need the market or competition to get richer, do we? We just need to make sure that wages are automatically increased.

When a baker bakes better bread and succeeds in selling it for twice the price, he adds value . He makes a better product and consumers are prepared to pay for it. Baker and consumer are content, and wealth is created as a result.

If the government decides to double the price of bread – as a way of ensuring better wages for bakers – no value is added. On the contrary, it is destroyed. Consumers must pay more for the same product without there being more demand or without a corresponding increase in quality. The result is the reduction of value.

This is also the case with the evolution of wages. An automatic wage increase has precisely the same effect: it does not add value. In a free market prices are generated by the confrontation of supply and demand. When rising wages are the result of a greater demand for labor, better-trained labor or more productive labor, value is added. Higher productivity adds value and, at the same time, justifies higher wages. Higher wages in themselves do not add value.

So, higher productivity leads to more wealth and that leads to higher wages? If that's true, then competition with low-wage countries must cause our wealth to decline!

Don't say low-wage countries, say low-productivity countries. The reason wages are lower there is because productivity is lower. Because people there can barely read and write, are less well educated or only speak one language.

If countries with lower wages can provide cheaper labor than we can, that benefits consumers and employees here. Consumers will have access to cheaper products. The money they will be able to save this way can be spent on products that are made here.

In fact, low-wage countries are a catalyst in the process of creative destruction. It is an illusion to try to counteract the process of disappearing sectors or industries. In the first place it is expensive to maintain non-competitive sectors by means of subsidies and special measures. Second, it is a natural process that has already existed for decades, even centuries: businesses come and businesses go. Sectors come and sectors go. Third: as long as the 'losing' sectors are protected, their employees will not be available to work in new and more promising sectors.

The employees here who lose their jobs through competition with low-wage countries are worthy of our attention and support. We have to make sure they are guided towards or retrained for jobs in sectors where we do have a competitive advantage.

But doesn't free trade result in a race to the bottom, in which working conditions will only get worse?
The opposite is true. In reality, we see a race to the top. Countries that compete internationally are forced to deliver better products and more added value every time.

When our productivity rises, we will no longer be able or willing to do certain jobs because they no longer seem worth the trouble. Someone with lower productivity will perform these jobs.

Why should a computer scientist stitch together T-shirts? With his knowledge of computers he can add a great deal more value in the IT-sector. Why should we oblige a commercial baker to knead his bread by hand? With his higher productivity he can add more value in his commercial bakery.

The least productive jobs today are already much more productive than the least productive jobs 20 years ago. The most productive jobs are becoming that much more productive. More education, more research and development and more training guarantee that both richer and poorer countries will continue to become increasingly productive. We all grow wealthier in this way.

Globalization means that businesses have to close their doors and jobs will disappear. It is high time we protected our own economy against foreign competition. Through protectionism, we can protect our own industries and keep jobs here....

Protectionism is the best way to destroy wealth. Protectionism is a conscious policy of denying foreign products access to domestic markets, for the sole reason that they are manufactured abroad. Whether the products are better or cheaper is irrelevant to protectionists. Protectionism is a particularly shortsighted policy, both for domestic consumers and for the sectors that are thought to be in need of protection.

Domestic consumers are denied access to imported products. The result is that consumers will have to pay higher prices and, on top of that, will have a more limited freedom of choice.

Domestic producers seem to be on the winning end in the short term. They are spared foreign competition and do not have to adapt. The final result, however, is that they will be lulled to sleep and become lazy: they will innovate less and will lose their competitive advantage.

Sooner or later, when the protectionist measures disappear, domestic industry will be the biggest loser. They will have been able to enjoy the cozy warmth of the hothouse temporarily, but will succumb to the freezing cold when they have to compete on their own strength once again.

Always this focus on wealth and growth. Why do we need growth, then?
All people, all over the world and throughout history, want but one thing: to improve their lot and that of their loved ones. This desire can be summed up in one word: progress. Or in other words: 'growth'. Or as Thomas Friedman said: "The basic human desire for a better life: a life with more choices as to what to eat, what to wear, where to live, where to travel, how to work, what to read, what to write and what to learn." That is progress. That is growth. Who are we to deny that to the rest of the world?

But if we keep growing, the earth will implode under the pressure of what will soon be ten billion people!
Replace 'ten' with 'one', 'two', or 'five' and you will find this theory has been around for a long time. Whether issued by Thomas Malthus, Garrett Hardin or the Club of Rome, reports on the imminent population explosion have been around for decades, even centuries.

What they all have in common is that they structurally underestimate the human capacity for innovation. The new technologies that will make our environmental and resource problems manageable will in fact arrive – as recent decades have shown. Since the earliest times, this has been what human beings do: use their brains and ingenuity to confront the challenges of their natural environment. There is nothing to suggest that human beings have suddenly lost this capacity.

Agricultural production in poorer countries does indeed have a lot of catching up to do. Access to fertilizers, better seeds, farming equipment and large-scale, more intensive cultivation are the only way to feed the growing population. The population of Africa will increase almost fourfold in the next century. Better technology, better farming techniques, but also more free market and better governance are also necessary to make a difference. Humanity already produces enough food to feed the entire population of the world. Storage, transportation and political or military conflicts are often the biggest problems in getting food to those who need it most.

The number of people that go hungry, in absolute figures, has dropped significantly in recent decades – and that against the background of a world population that has kept growing in the mean time.

What is needed to help the poorest people on the planet is often not more food, but better food. Iodine added to salt, cheap disinfectants for water, iron supplements in food.... These are small steps that can improve the lives of the poorest among us. The faster their standard of living improves, the faster birth rates will decline and the world population will stabilize.

People are, increasingly, urban animals. For the first time in human history, more people live in cities than outside of cities. While life in cities used to be synonymous with disease, deprivation and poverty, life in cities today is often better than ever before and better than in the countryside. More jobs, more access to education, better food and medical care. Cities are the places where ideas are exchanged and wealth is created.

The world population is going through a couple of centuries of demographic transition. A high birth rate is a sign of poverty; a low birth rate is a sign of affluence. More growth and more affluence are expected in the future, and so we can also expect that the world population will reach its peak sooner rather than later.

The income differences between rich countries and developing countries have increased in the last century. Nevertheless, it is not only the rich countries that have become richer – the poor countries have also become richer.

In the past few years the growth rates of developing countries and emerging markets have been structurally higher than in the West. Everything indicates that this will remain the case for some time. In terms of technology and levels of productivity, they are gaining on the West at breakneck speed. In many cases one might even compare the process to a game of leapfrog, in which developing countries simply skip over several steps at once. Many countries could take advantage of portable computers right away, without having to start off with our computers from the 1950s. Another example is that many countries immediately started using mobile phones and skipped over the stage of fixed landlines.

At the same time, the difference between the richest countries and the poorest countries in terms of child mortality, life expectancy, and literacy continues to decrease. Life expectancy will increase even faster in developing countries than in rich countries in the coming decades. Child mortality will also decrease faster in developing countries than in rich countries. We will be more numerous than ever before, just as we will be freer, healthier, older, and wealthier than ever before.

Stabilization of the world population or not: developing countries are never going to catch up to our standard of living. We need to devote more effort to the redistribution of wealth.

If everything is going to turn out all right in the end, why are people always predicting the end of the economic, demographic, or financial world?

Pessimism and cynicism are fashionable. Today, an optimist is all too often accused of being a poorly informed pessimist. An optimist or a realist has to present much better arguments than a pessimist. It is enough for a pessimist to say, "everything will explode." The optimist, by contrast, is expected to refute this with arguments.

Agreed, but I read everywhere that things are deteriorating on planet earth. Several books today point to the impending decline of humanity and planet alike:

» *The Population Bomb* by Paul Ehrlich
» *Limits to Growth* by the Club of Rome
» *Collapse* by Jared Diamond

Try reading some other books for a change:

» *The Skeptical Environmentalist* by Bjørn Lomborg
» *The Rational Optimist* by Matt Ridley
» *It's Getting Better all the Time* by Stephen Moore and Julian L. Simon
» *The Plundered Planet* by Paul Collier
» *Poor Economics* by Abhijit V. Banerjee and Esther Duflo

OK: technology and progress will save us. Still, I hear all sorts of rumors about disasters, global warming and a world that is heading in the worst possible direction. Where will these miracle technologies come from?

Millions of scientists and entrepreneurs around the world are today working on the solutions of tomorrow. Innovation is the engine of progress and greater affluence.

For those who want to stay abreast with all these developments, there are plenty of ways of staying up to date:
Wired
Scientific American
National Geographic
Popular Science
Lowtechmagazine
Technology Quarterly, a supplement to The Economist

Publications like these are the best medicine for too much pessimism. They offer a glimpse of what is possible, not what holds us back. In a climate in which we are constantly being told what cannot be done and what is going wrong, there is nothing better than a good scientific article to cure what ails you.

"One science article a day keeps pessimism away...."

I'm totally convinced. What can I do to help better the world?
» Help ensure growth, both at home and in emerging markets and developing countries.
» Become an entrepreneur and help work on the solutions of tomorrow for the problems of today.
» Become an engineer. Study chemistry, biology, computer science, medicine or physics.
» Understand that wealth must always, always be created before it can be shared.
» Understand that free markets are the guarantee of the most possible wealth for the most possible people.
» Understand, finally, that growth and wealth are not legislated. They come into being where there is freedom to innovate, to compete and to create.

Thanks

Every idea has many fathers. With this book it is no different. It is the result of years of sustained interest in everything that is happening economically, socially, and politically. Many, many people who crossed my path have directly or indirectly influenced the ideas in this book. Some agreed with those ideas wholeheartedly, others not at all. Most found themselves somewhere in the middle. Nevertheless, there are a number of people in particular I would like to thank.

First and foremost, Tom and Jeroen – the best friends anyone could hope for, going on a quarter of a century now. Their endless and uninterrupted interest in everything happening in the world – economically, socially, historically and politically – has stimulated me all these years. To keep thinking, to keep studying and to keep writing. Without them, this book would never have come into being.

Stefaan Van Langendonck, Ivo Bosteels, Bart Van Craeynest, and Jeroen Vandamme – four (ex-) colleagues to whom I am particularly grateful. With them I have been able to constantly test all manner of ideas over the years. They were always ready for a good discussion and always had new arguments and visions that challenged me and got me thinking.

Herman Daems, Paul De Grauwe and Thomas Lambert – for the support and stimulating exchange of ideas.

Ignace Van Doorselaere – for the inspiration, and for his idea about the four quadrants in chapter 10.

A special word of thanks is due to my many stimulating colleagues at BNP Paribas Fortis. Their constant and many-sided questions, observations and discussions about world events inspire me every day afresh to keep thinking about how everything could be better.

Finally, I am especially grateful to the two reading committees. They have wrestled through this work in a very short time and given me a lot of useful and interesting feedback. I would like to thank by name Peter Frans Anthonissen, Lieven Cuvelier, Stijn Decock, Bart Van Craeynest, Benedicte Stockman, Fred Schalckens, Andreas Tirez, Johan Van Overtveldt and Jean Van den Eynde. Marc Vanheukelen I would like to thank specially for his insights and observations. I am grateful to them all for the help, inspiration, improvements, and suggestions that have made this book possible in its present form. All remaining errors, mistakes, lack of nuance – or too much of the same – are entirely my own responsibility.

This book was written in my own name. In no way does it represent the position, points of view, opinions or analyses of BNP Paribas Fortis or the BNP Paribas Group. They cannot be held responsible in any way for the contents of this book.

Bibliography

Acemoglu, D. & Robinson, J.A. (2012). *Why Nations Fail - The origins of power, prosperity and poverty*, London: Profile Books.

Antonioni, P. & Flynn, S.M. (2011). *Economics for Dummies*, Hoboken (New Jersey): Wiley.

Apostolides, A. et al. (2008). *English agricultural output and labour productivity, 1250-1850: some preliminary estimates*; Project: Reconstructing the National Income of Britain and Holland, c.1270/1500 to 1850, funded by the Leverhulme Trust, Ref. F/00215AR.

Banerjee, A. & Duflo, E. (2011). *Poor Economics - Barefoot Hedge-fund Managers, DIY Doctors and the Surprising Truth about Life on Less Than $1 a Day*, London: Penguin Books Ltd.

Bastiat, F. (1845). *Sophismes Économiques*.

Berners-Lee, M. (2010). *How Bad are Bananas? - The Carbon Footprint of Everything*, London: Profile Books Ltd.

Behravesh, N. (2009), *Spin-Free Economics - A No-Nonsense Nonpartisan Guide to Today's Global Economic Debates*, New York: McGraw-Hill Books.

Boston Consulting Group (2013), *Collateral Damage - Ending the Era of Ponzi Finance - Ten Steps Developed Economies Must Take*, The Boston Consulting Group

Broadberry, S. & Klein, A. (2011). *Aggregate and per capita GDP in Europe, 1870-2000: Continental, regional and national data with changing boundaries*; Collaborative Project HI-POD supported by the European Commission's 7th Framework Programme for Research .

Cincotta, R.P., Engelman, R. & Anastasion, D. (2003). *The Security Demographic - Population and Civil Conflict after the Cold War*, Population Action International

Cincotta, R.P. (2004). The Next Steps for Environment, Population, and Security - Demographic Security Comes of Age. *ECSP Report Issue 10*.

Cincotta, P. & Leahy, E. (2007). Population age structure and its relation to civil conflict: a graphic metric. *ECSP Report Issue 12*.

Cincotta, R.P. (2008-2009). New Directions in Demographic Security - Half a Chance: Youth Bulges and Transitions to Liberal Democracy. *ECSP Report Issue 13*.

Collier, P. (2010). *Plundered Planet – How to Reconcile Prosperity with Nature*, London: Penguin Books Ltd.

Conway, E. (2009). *50 economics ideas you really need to know*, London: Quercus Publishing Plc.

Cutler, D., Deaton, A. & Lleras-Muney, A. (2005). *The Determinants of Mortality*, Department of Economics, Harvard University – Woodrow Wilson School and Department of Economics, Princeton University.

Deaton, A. (2003). Health, Inequality, and Economic Development. *Journal of Economic Literature Vol. XLI March 2003*, pp. 113-158.

De Borger, B. & Proost, S.(2006). *Prijshervormingen in de transportsector, pendel en arbeidsmarkt*, in *Mobiliteit en Grootstedenbeleid*. Vlaams Wetenschappelijk Economisch Congres, pp. 257 – 306.

Dollar, David & Kraay, Aart (2002). *Growth Is Good for the Poor*, World Bank.

Dollar, D., Kleineberg, T. & Kraay, A. (2013), *Growth Still Is Good For The Poor*, World Bank.

Federal Reserve Bank of Dallas (1992). *The Churn – The Paradox of Progress*, published in the annual report.

Food and Agriculture Organization of the United Nations (FAO) (2012). *The State of Food and Agriculture*.

Fraser Institute (2012), *Economic Freedom of the World – 2012 Annual Report*.

Friedman, B.M. (2005). *The moral consequences of economic growth*, New York: Vintage Books.

Friedman, M. (2002), *Capitalism and Freedom*, Chicago: The University of Chicago Press.

Gordon, Robert J. (2012), *Is US economic growth over? Faltering innovation confronts the six headwinds*; NBER Working Paper Series, Working Paper 18315.

Gordon, R.J. (2012). Is US economic growth over? Faltering innovation confronts the six headwinds. *Policy Insight no. 63*, Centre for Economic Policy Research.

Hardin, G. (1974). Living on a Lifeboat (A reprint from BioScience, October 1974). *The Social Contract*, autumn 2001.

Hayek, F.A. (2010). *The Road to Serfdom*, London: Routledge Classics.

Hazlitt, H. (1979). *Economics in One Lesson – The Shortest & Surest Way to Understand Basic Economics*, New York: Three Rivers Press.

Heckelman, J.C. (2007). Symposium – Explaining the Rain: The Rise and Decline of Nations after 25 Years. *Southern Economic Journal 2007, 74(1)*, pp. 18-33.

Helpman, E. (2004), *The Mystery of Economic Growth*, Cambridge (Massachusetts): Harvard University Press.

International Labour Organisation (2007). *Working Time Around the World - Trends in Working Hours, Laws and Policies in a Global Perspective*, London: Routledge.

International Monetary Fund (2013). *World Economic Outlook*, April 2013.

Kay, J. (2003). *The Truth About Markets - Why some nations are rich but most remain poor*, London: Penguin Books Ltd.

Lam, D. (2011). How the World Survived the Population Bomb: Lessons from 50 Years of Extraordinary Demographic History. *Population Studies Center Research Report 11-743.*

Lee, R. (2003). The Demographic Transition: Three Centuries of Fundamental Change. *Journal of Economic Perspectives, volume 17, nr. 4, autumn 2003*, pp. 167-190.

Lester, S. (2013). Genetically Modified Foods and the Limits of Trade Agreements. *Huffington Post* 23/05/2013.

Lester, S. (2013). Transatlantic Regulatory Trade Barriers. *Huffington Post* 12/07/2013.

Lomborg, B. (2012). *Environmental Alarmism, Then and Now - The Club of Rome's Problem - and Ours*, Foreign Affairs.

Lopez, J.H. (2011). *Pro-poor growth: a review of what we know (and of what we don't)*; Working Paper prepared in the context of the 'Pro-poor Growth' program sponsored by the World Bank's PREM Poverty Group.

Maddison, A. (2007) *Contours of the World Economy, 1-2030 AD - Essays in Macro-Economic History*, Oxford University Press.

Moore, S. & Simon, J.L. (2000). *It's Getting Better All the Time - 100 Greatest Trends of the Last 100 Years*, Washington: Cato Institute.

Nelson, G. (2013). Toyota puts high beams on headlight regulation - Petition says rules stifle technology that could save lives. *Automotive News 13/05/2013.*

Norberg, J. (2003). *In Defense of Global Capitalism*, Washington: Cato Institute.

Norberg, J. (2008). The Klein Doctrine: The Rise of Disaster Polemics. *Cato Institute, Briefing Paper no. 102, 14/05/2008,*

Nozick, R. (1998). Why Do Intellectuals Oppose Capitalism? *Cato Institute, Policy Report January/February 1998.*

OESO (2012). *The challenge of promoting youth employment in the G20 countries.*

Olson, M. (1982). *The Rise and Decline of Nations - Economic Growth, Stagflation, and Social Rigidities*, New Haven: Yale University Press.

Ottens, N. (2011). Did Government End Child Labor? Atlantic Sentinel, blog Free Market Fundamentalist.

Pirie, M. (2012). *Economics Made Simple - How money, trade and markets really work*, Petersfield: Harriman House Ltd.

Radford, R.A. (1945). The Economic Organization of a POW Camp. *Economica*.

Riley, B. (2013). Egyptians Need More Than a Change of Presidents. *The Heritage Foundation (Leadership for America)*, 09/07/2013.

Simms, A. (2013), *Cancel the Apocalypse - The New Path to Prosperity*, London: Little, Brown.Schuettinger, R.L. & Butler, E.F. (1979). Forty Centuries of Wage and Price Controls: How Not To Fight Inflation. *The Heritage Foundation*, distributed by Caroline House, Publishers, Inc.

Smith, L. (2010). *The New North - The World in 2050*, London: Profile Books Ltd.

Tupy, M.L. (2010). Africa Needs Free Market Economies. *Global Post* 06/02/2010.

Unicef (2012). *Levels & Trends in Child Mortality - Report 2012*, United Nations.

United Nations (1999). *The World at Six Billion*.

United Nations (2011). *World Population Prospects: The 2010 Revision*.

United Nations (2013). *World Population Prospects: The 2012 Revision, Key Findings and Advance Tables*.

United Nations (2012). *World Urbanization Prospects: The 2011 Revision, Highlights*.

United Nations (2004). *World Population to 2300*.

Von Mises, L.(2004). *The Free Market and Its Enemies: Pseudo-Science, Socialism, and Inflation*, Foundation for Economic Education.

Watson, R. (2012). *Future Files - A brief history of the next 50 years*, London/ Boston: Nicholas Brealey Publishing.

World Bank (2011). *Rising Global Interest in Farmland*.